THE
ARTISANAL
KITCHEN

PARTY
CAKES

ALSO IN THIS SERIES

The Artisanal Kitchen: Perfect Pasta

The Artisanal Kitchen: Perfect Pizza at Home

The Artisanal Kitchen: Vegetables the Italian Way

The Artisanal Kitchen: Holiday Cocktails

The Artisanal Kitchen: Holiday Cookies

The Artisanal Kitchen: Party Food

The Artisanal Kitchen: Baking for Breakfast

The Artisanal Kitchen: Sweets & Treats

THE ARTISANAL KITCHEN

PARTY
CAKES

36 DECADENT CREATIONS
for FESTIVE OCCASIONS

CHERYL DAY AND GRIFFITH DAY

ARTISAN | NEW YORK

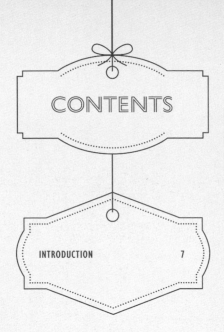

CONTENTS

INTRODUCTION 7

CHOCOLATE HEAVEN WITH 17
CHOCOLATE BUTTERCREAM

COCONUT CAKE WITH 21
COCONUT BUTTERCREAM

RED VELVET CAKE WITH 25
CREAM CHEESE FROSTING

HUMMINGBIRD CAKE WITH 29
CREAM CHEESE FROSTING

CARROT CAKE WITH 32
SPICED CREAM CHEESE FROSTING

CAKETTE PARTY CAKE WITH 34
ITALIAN MERINGUE BUTTERCREAM

CARAMEL CAKE WITH 43
SALTED CARAMEL FROSTING

CHOCOLATE CREAM CAKE WITH 51
DARK CHOCOLATE GANACHE

JANIE Q'S LEMON CAKE WITH 56
LEMON MERINGUE BUTTERCREAM

ALABAMA LANE CAKE 61

BROWN SUGAR BUNDT CAKE WITH 65
BUTTERSCOTCH GLAZE

DEEP, DARK FLOURLESS 69
CHOCOLATE CAKE

SPICE CAKE WITH 71
BUTTERSCOTCH ICING

MEXICAN SPICE CAKE WITH
CHOCOLATE GLAZE   74

ANGEL FOOD CAKE WITH
WHIPPED CREAM AND BERRIES   76

COCOA-COLA CAKE WITH
CHOCOLATE ICING   81

CLEMENTINE POUND CAKE WITH
CHOCOLATE HONEY GLAZE   83

LEMON POPPY SEED CAKE WITH
LEMON GLAZE   87

PINEAPPLE UPSIDE-DOWN CAKE   89

BABY CAKES WITH
VANILLA MERINGUE BUTTERCREAM   93

FESTIVE YULE LOG   98

RESOURCES   105
INDEX   108

INTRODUCTION

Celebrations call for baking. Whether it's a birthday, a baby shower, or Christmas, who doesn't want a homemade cake to help mark the special day? And the wonderful thing about cakes is that there's the perfect one for any occasion. Hummingbird Cake with Cream Cheese Frosting (page 29) is a great way to mark the arrival of a new baby, a birthday party is all the more cheerful with Chocolate Heaven with Chocolate Buttercream (page 17), and a Festive Yule Log (page 98) will brighten any holiday buffet. Cakes bring a certain magic to your table and make everyone around it feel special.

THE METHOD TO THE MAGIC

There's a mystique that surrounds baking. Even after all these years, Griff and I remain fascinated by the process of mixing just a few simple ingredients together and creating something wonderful. The fact of the matter is, though, there is a method to the magic, and it is accessible to everyone.

Baking requires practice and patience. It is a science, and learning how to measure your ingredients properly and understanding the details of a recipe will make you a better baker. We have all had the experience of creating a tough cake that could be mistaken for a floor tile. You feel inadequate when a recipe doesn't work out.

While baking can be simple and fun, it does require mastering techniques that will give you those delicious results we all want to achieve. However, once you learn the fundamentals and how to use all of your senses, you can bake for your family and friends and earn bragging rights for your delicious victories.

Here are some of the fundamentals I adhere to.

GET IT TOGETHER

The French term *mise en place* means, literally, to "put in place." It makes a big difference to have all of your ingredients measured and ready to go before you start to mix. So do like the TV chefs do and assemble your ingredients before you're ready to bake.

Always begin by reading your recipe through to make sure you have a clear understanding of the process involved, as well as of all the ingredients and tools needed. For instance, cake recipes usually call for room-temperature ingredients, and pies and pastries require some cold ingredients. And in baking, as in many other things, timing is of the essence. The last thing you want to do is have to run around the kitchen preparing your cake pans or getting your eggs up to room temperature after you've started mixing.

Start with a clean kitchen and have everything prepped to go. Once you are organized and have your tools ready, you will have the confidence to mix and bake like a pro.

TEMPERATURE MATTERS

Always bring your ingredients to the temperature called for in the recipe before you begin baking. This is what my grandmother taught me so many years ago, and I assure you, if you follow this rule, you'll get the best results.

When a recipe calls for eggs at room temperature, it is critical that you bring them to room temperature. Here is why: if the eggs are too cold when added to your perfectly creamed butter, the butter will seize up, deflating the air bubbles that you have created, and the batter will resist mixing completely. If that happens, the air bubbles will not expand during baking and the result will be a flat, dense cake, not one with the fluffy and tender crumb that you want. I know this from experience.

I understand being in a hurry, believe me! When I've got five or six things to get out for the bakery's opening and special orders to get done by midday, I look for good shortcuts. Here's a quick and easy way to bring eggs up to room temperature: put the whole eggs in a small bowl of hot water and swish them around for about 1 minute, being careful not to bang their delicate shells against one another.

Bringing butter to room temperature is important too. If you have an instant-read thermometer, the proper temperature is between 65° and 67°F, still cool but not cold. You can either pull the butter out of the refrigerator 30 minutes or so before you are ready to bake or cut it into small cubes to speed the process of bringing it to room temperature.

A few visual and tactile clues can also help you determine the proper temperature. You should be able to make an indentation with your finger on the surface of the butter, but the butter should be slightly firm, not hard—and definitely not squishy. If the butter gets too warm, label it with the date, then return it to the refrigerator for future use in something that does not require creaming. Start again with fresh butter.

Another point about temperature: an oven thermometer is one of the most important tools in a baker's kit (see page 14). If the oven is not hot enough, rising will be inhibited, and that means flat cakes. Use an oven thermometer to make sure your oven has reached the desired temperature and is calibrated correctly. And always preheat your oven for at least 20 minutes (30 is preferable) so it reaches the proper temperature.

THE INGREDIENTS ARE KEY

It is important to have a clear understanding of the role each ingredient plays in the baking process. In baking, it's never okay to substitute ingredients or to skip over steps and think it will all work out in the end.

Take the unassuming egg. Eggs perform so many important functions in baked goods. They leaven, thicken, moisturize, and enhance flavor. Whole eggs, as well as just yolks, act as great emulsifiers. The lecithin in egg yolks binds fats and water, which normally resist each other. Eggs and oil can become mayonnaise, or the key components in the moist texture and delicate crumb of a Chocolate Heaven cake (page 17).

Eggs also provide structure. When egg whites are whipped to stiff peaks and folded into a batter, the air trapped in the whites will expand in the heat of the oven during baking, acting as the leavening agent for such light and airy desserts as Deep, Dark Flourless Chocolate Cake (page 69).

Baking soda and baking powder are both leaveners as well. They create chemical reactions in a batter to force air bubbles to expand during the baking process. Baking soda requires the presence of an acid, such as sour cream, buttermilk, molasses, non-alkalized cocoa powder, or brown sugar (which contains molasses), to name a few. Baking powder reacts without the presence of acid. Once it is combined with a liquid, such as milk, it releases carbon dioxide, creating air bubbles that cause a cake layer to rise.

Baking powder made with aluminum compounds has a chemical aftertaste. We use aluminum-free baking powder in all of our recipes that call for this ingredient. It may cost a bit more, but you will notice the difference in the way your baked goods taste. Aluminum-free baking powder is available in the natural foods section in supermarkets or online from King Arthur Flour (see Resources, page 105).

MEASURING FLOUR

When you measure flour, you want to first loosen up or fluff the flour a bit with your measuring cup or a spoon. We recommend storing flour in a canister rather than in a flour sack so that you have plenty of room to dip and scoop. Spoon the flour into your measuring cup until it is heaping, then sweep a straight edge, such as the back of a butter knife, across the top to level the flour. Do not tap the cup to settle the flour.

CREAMING BUTTER

To produce the perfect texture in cakes, you must master the art of creaming butter, the foundation of so many recipes. Most cake recipes start with the words "cream the butter and sugar" or "beat the butter and sugar together," often without any explanation of what that actually means. They fail to tell you that if you don't do this step properly, the result can be disastrous. If your butter is too cold, it will not whip properly. If it is too soft, it will not retain air. The most important factor in creaming butter and sugar is the temperature of the butter (see "Temperature Matters" on page 8).

When a recipe calls for creaming butter and sugar, you want to beat the soft-ened butter and sugar together until the mixture is light in both color and tex-ture; this incorporates air into the structure. (We've included time estimates in all the recipes to give you a sense of how long this step will take.) This is where science comes into play. The creaming process aerates the butter; air bubbles are literally forced into the butter mixture. These air bubbles expand during baking, making cookies light and tender and cakes delicate and but-tery. Once you master this technique, you will be amazed to see what a differ-ence it makes. Your cakes will have a light, delicate crumb.

THE BAKER'S TOOL KIT

Just as a carpenter needs a hammer and nails to frame a wall, the baker requires some essential tools to create successful cakes.

APPLIANCES

Blender or coffee grinder
4- to 5-quart stand mixer

Handheld mixer

POTS, PANS, AND BAKING PANS

6- to 8-quart heavy-bottomed
  nonreactive stockpot
2- to 3-quart heavy-bottomed
  nonreactive saucepan
10-inch cast-iron skillet
10-inch Bundt pan
10-inch tube pan
10-inch round cake pan
Three 6-inch round cake pans

Six 4-inch round cake pans
Three 9-inch round cake pans
8-inch square baking pan
9-by-13-inch baking pan
9-inch springform pan
9-by-5-inch loaf pan
Two or more 12-by-17-inch
  rimmed baking sheets

UTENSILS AND OTHER TOOLS

Candy thermometer
Dry measuring cups
Fine-mesh sieve
Heat-resistant silicone spatulas
Heat-resistant spoons

Ice cream scoops—small
  (39 mm/1½ tablespoons) and large
  (52 mm/3 tablespoons)
Instant-read thermometer
Kitchen scale

Kitchen shears
Liquid measuring cups
   (the kind with pouring spouts)
Measuring spoons
Offset metal spatulas: small,
   medium, and large
1-inch round cookie cutter
Oven mitts

Oven thermometer
Parchment paper
Pastry bags and tips
Silicone baking mats (Silpats)
Silicone-bristle pastry brush
Timer
Wire cooling racks
Wire whisk

A PEEK INSIDE OUR SPICE CABINET

Most of these seasonings are readily available from your local grocer, but some we purchase from the spice vendors listed in our Resources section (page 105).

Allspice (ground)
Cardamom (ground and pods)
Cayenne pepper
Cinnamon (ground and sticks)
Cloves (ground)
Cream of tartar

Fine sea salt (see Tip)
Fleur de sel
Ginger (ground)
Mace
Nutmeg (ground and whole)
Rosemary

TIP: At the bakery, we use only fine sea salt (*sel de mer*) and fleur de sel, a more coarsely ground finishing salt from France. We like the good flavor they add to both sweet and savory dishes. However, you can substitute table salt in any of the recipes that call for fine sea salt, using the same measurement.

CHOCOLATE HEAVEN WITH CHOCOLATE BUTTERCREAM

SERVES 10 TO 12

This cake was the first thing I learned to bake with my grandmother. It was, and still is, the best cake I have ever tasted. The Scharffen Berger chocolate we use at the bakery puts a new spin on a nostalgic cake, and a hint of strong coffee adds another flavor dimension. Topped with a decadent buttercream frosting, this cake is everything you want a chocolate cake to be, and a sweet finale for any special occasion.

3 CUPS CAKE FLOUR (NOT SELF-RISING)

4 CUPS SUGAR

1½ TEASPOONS BAKING SODA

1 TEASPOON FINE SEA SALT

9 OUNCES UNSWEETENED CHOCOLATE, FINELY CHOPPED

2 CUPS HOT FRESHLY BREWED COFFEE

1 TABLESPOON PURE VANILLA EXTRACT

4 LARGE EGGS, AT ROOM TEMPERATURE

1 CUP CANOLA OIL

1 CUP SOUR CREAM, AT ROOM TEMPERATURE

1 RECIPE CHOCOLATE BUTTERCREAM (RECIPE FOLLOWS)

Position a rack in the lower third of the oven and preheat the oven to 350°F. Butter three 9-inch round cake pans, then line the bottoms with parchment and butter it as well. Lightly dust the pans with flour, tapping the pans on the counter to shake out the excess.

In the bowl of a stand mixer fitted with the paddle attachment (or in a large mixing bowl, using a handheld mixer), combine the flour, sugar, baking soda, and salt. Let the mixer run on low speed for 2 to 3 minutes to aerate the flour.

continued

Meanwhile, put the chocolate in a medium bowl and pour in the hot coffee and vanilla. Let stand for about 2 minutes to melt the chocolate, then stir until smooth.

In another medium bowl, whisk the eggs and oil together until thick, satiny, and light in color. Whisk in the sour cream, being careful not to overmix; leave some visible streaks of white. Pour in the melted chocolate mixture and mix until just combined. Add the chocolate–sour cream mixture to the dry ingredients in thirds, mixing on medium speed until well blended.

Remove the bowl from the mixer and, using a rubber spatula, incorporate any ingredients hiding at the bottom of the bowl, making sure the batter is completely mixed.

Divide the batter evenly among the prepared pans and smooth the tops with a spatula. Tap the pans firmly on the counter to remove any air bubbles from the batter.

Bake for 40 to 50 minutes, until the center of a cake springs back a little when touched and a cake tester inserted in the center of a cake comes out clean. The cakes will be a deep, dark chocolate brown with slight cracks on top. Let the cakes cool for 20 minutes, then remove from the pans and cool completely on a wire rack.

To assemble the cake: Level the tops of two of the cake layers with a serrated knife so they are flat. Place one layer cut side down on a serving plate (you can keep the edges of the plate clean by sliding strips of parchment under the cake while you frost it). Using an offset spatula, spread the top of the layer with a big dollop of frosting. Place the second layer cut side down on top of the first and spread the top with another big dollop of frosting. Place the final layer on top, right side up, and frost the top and sides with the remaining frosting, making big luscious swirls with the spatula.

The cake can be stored in an airtight container at room temperature for up to 2 days.

Chocolate Buttercream

9 OUNCES SEMISWEET CHOCOLATE, CHOPPED

¾ POUND (3 STICKS) UNSALTED BUTTER, AT ROOM TEMPERATURE

2 TABLESPOONS WHOLE MILK

1 TEASPOON PURE VANILLA EXTRACT

2½ TO 3 CUPS CONFECTIONERS' SUGAR, SIFTED

Put the chocolate in a heatproof bowl set over a simmering saucepan of water (do not let the bottom of the bowl touch the water) and stir occasionally until the chocolate is completely melted. Set the chocolate aside to cool to room temperature.

In the bowl of a stand mixer fitted with the paddle attachment (or in a medium mixing bowl, using a handheld mixer), beat the butter on medium speed until smooth and creamy. Add the milk, mixing until completely blended. Add the cooled chocolate and mix until completely incorporated, 2 to 3 minutes, scraping down the sides of the bowl with a rubber spatula as necessary. Add the vanilla and beat just until mixed. With the mixer on low speed, gradually add 2½ cups confectioners' sugar and continue beating, adding more sugar as needed, until you reach a creamy, silky frosting consistency.

The frosting can be stored in an airtight container at room temperature for up to 2 days.

COCONUT CAKE WITH COCONUT BUTTERCREAM

SERVES 10 TO 12

This snowy beauty is an elegant dessert to take to a party. A Southern standard, it was the first thing I made for Griff after he moved to Savannah. The shreds of delicate coconut atop the frosting are the perfect balance to the light and moist cake. Add one of our delicious simple syrups (see page 24) to make each bite one to remember.

3 CUPS UNBLEACHED ALL-PURPOSE FLOUR

½ TEASPOON BAKING SODA

1 TEASPOON BAKING POWDER, PREFERABLY ALUMINUM-FREE

¼ TEASPOON GROUND CARDAMOM

½ TEASPOON FINE SEA SALT

¾ CUP CREAM OF COCONUT, SUCH AS COCO LOPEZ

1½ TEASPOONS PURE VANILLA EXTRACT

1½ TEASPOONS PURE ALMOND EXTRACT

¾ POUND (3 STICKS) UNSALTED BUTTER, AT ROOM TEMPERATURE

2 CUPS SUGAR

6 LARGE EGGS, AT ROOM TEMPERATURE

1 RECIPE COCONUT BUTTERCREAM (RECIPE FOLLOWS)

3 CUPS SWEETENED FLAKED COCONUT

Position a rack in the lower third of the oven and preheat the oven to 350°F. Butter two 9-inch round cake pans and lightly dust with flour, tapping the pans on the counter to shake out the excess.

Sift together the flour, baking soda, baking powder, cardamom, and salt; set aside. In a large measuring cup or a small bowl, stir together the cream of coconut, ¼ cup water, the vanilla, and the almond extract.

continued

In the bowl of a stand mixer fitted with the paddle attachment (or in a large mixing bowl, using a handheld mixer), cream the butter and sugar together on medium-high speed for 3 to 5 minutes, until light and fluffy. Add the eggs one at a time, beating well after each addition and scraping down the sides of the bowl with a rubber spatula as necessary.

With the mixer on low speed, add the flour mixture in thirds, alternating with the cream of coconut mixture and beginning and ending with the flour, mixing just until combined; scrape down the sides of the bowl with a rubber spatula as necessary.

Divide the batter evenly between the prepared pans and smooth the tops with a spatula. Tap the pans firmly on the counter to remove any air bubbles from the batter. Bake for 45 to 50 minutes, until a cake tester inserted in the center of a cake comes out clean. Let cool for 20 minutes, then remove the cakes from the pans and cool completely on a wire rack.

To assemble the cake: Level the top of one of the cake layers with a serrated knife so it is flat. Place the layer cut side down on a serving plate (you can keep the edges of the plate clean by sliding strips of parchment under the cake while you frost it). Using an offset spatula, spread the top of the layer with a big dollop of frosting. Sprinkle about ½ cup of the coconut on top. Place the second layer on top, right side up, and frost the top and sides with the remaining frosting, making swirls with the spatula. Sprinkle some of the remaining coconut on top of the cake and press the rest onto the sides.

The cake can be stored in an airtight container at room temperature for up to 2 days.

Coconut Buttercream

MAKES ABOUT 6 CUPS

½ CUP ALL-PURPOSE FLOUR

2 CUPS WHOLE MILK

2 TEASPOONS PURE VANILLA EXTRACT

2 TEASPOONS COCONUT EXTRACT

1 POUND (4 STICKS) UNSALTED BUTTER, AT ROOM TEMPERATURE

2 CUPS CONFECTIONERS' SUGAR

Combine the flour, ½ cup of the milk, the vanilla, and the coconut extract in a small saucepan and whisk until blended. Set the pan over medium heat and gradually add the remaining 1½ cups milk, whisking constantly. Cook the mixture, whisking, until it comes to a low boil, then reduce the heat to low and continue to whisk until the mixture begins to thicken and starts to "burp," 2 to 3 minutes.

Transfer the mixture to a small heatproof bowl and stir it occasionally as it cools to keep it lump-free. (If you do get a few lumps, don't worry—you can whisk the mixture to dissolve the lumps, or pass it through a fine-mesh sieve.) Set the mixture aside to cool to room temperature. (You can put it in the refrigerator for 10 minutes to speed up the process.)

In the bowl of a stand mixer fitted with the whisk attachment (or in a large bowl, using a handheld mixer), whip the butter on medium speed until soft and creamy, 2 to 3 minutes. Gradually add the confectioners' sugar and beat on high speed until light and fluffy, 5 to 7 minutes.

Gradually add the milk mixture, then increase the speed to medium-high and whip until the frosting is light and fluffy, scraping down the bottom and sides of the bowl as necessary with a rubber spatula to make sure the frosting is thoroughly mixed.

The frosting can be stored in an airtight container at room temperature for up to 2 days.

HOW TO MAKE
SIMPLE SYRUP

Adding a glaze of simple syrup to a cake provides an element of surprise. It moistens the cake and, if you make one of the variations, gives another dimension to the flavor. To make simple syrup, combine 1 cup water and 1 cup sugar in a small saucepan and heat over medium heat, stirring, until the sugar completely dissolves. Bring the syrup to a boil and boil for 3 to 5 minutes, until it turns golden. Let cool, and refrigerate in an airtight container for up to 2 weeks.

For variations, add almond, coconut, vanilla, coffee, or rum extract to taste. If you want a citrus flavor, substitute 1 cup fresh lemon juice for the water.

To use the syrup, poke several holes in each cake layer using a toothpick, and brush the simple syrup generously on the cake layers. Allow the syrup to soak in for a few minutes before assembling and frosting the cake.

You can also use simple syrup to sugar fruit for decorating cakes and cupcakes. Simply brush it on clean, dry fruit and roll in granulated sugar. Set the fruit aside to dry on a parchment-lined pan.

RED VELVET CAKE WITH CREAM CHEESE FROSTING

SERVES 10 TO 12

This cake helped to open a lot of doors for us. Jamie and Bobby Deen filmed the Christmas episode of their Food Network show, *Road Tasted*, at our bakery a few years after we opened. We made red velvet cupcakes with the boys. A lot of folks who've never had this scarlet lady ask what it tastes like. We tell them it has a hint of chocolate with a sweet, tangy finish from the cream cheese frosting.

3 CUPS CAKE FLOUR (NOT SELF-RISING)

1 TEASPOON BAKING SODA

1½ TEASPOONS DUTCH-PROCESSED COCOA POWDER, SIFTED

8 TABLESPOONS (1 STICK) UNSALTED BUTTER, AT ROOM TEMPERATURE

1 CUP VEGETABLE OIL

2 CUPS SUGAR

4 LARGE EGGS, AT ROOM TEMPERATURE

ONE 1-OUNCE BOTTLE RED FOOD COLORING

1 TEASPOON CIDER VINEGAR

1 TEASPOON PURE VANILLA EXTRACT

1 CUP BUTTERMILK

1 RECIPE CREAM CHEESE FROSTING (RECIPE FOLLOWS)

Position a rack in the lower third of the oven and preheat the oven to 350°F. Butter two 9-inch round cake pans, then line the bottoms with parchment and butter it as well. Lightly dust the pans with flour, tapping the pans on the counter to shake out the excess.

Sift together the cake flour, baking soda, and cocoa; set aside.

continued

In the bowl of a stand mixer fitted with the paddle attachment (or in a large mixing bowl, using a handheld mixer), cream the butter, oil, and sugar together on medium-low to medium speed for 5 to 7 minutes, until very pale and thick. Add the eggs one at a time, beating well after each addition. Add the food coloring, vinegar, and vanilla and mix for 1 to 2 minutes. Add the sifted dry ingredients in thirds, alternating with the buttermilk, beginning and ending with the flour, scraping down the sides of the bowl as necessary. Mix for another 1 to 2 minutes.

Remove the bowl from the mixer and, using a rubber spatula, incorporate any ingredients hiding at the bottom of the bowl, making sure the batter is completely mixed. Divide the batter evenly between the prepared pans and gently smooth the tops with a spatula. Tap the pans firmly on the counter to remove any air bubbles from the batter.

Bake for 40 to 50 minutes, until a cake tester inserted in the center of a cake comes out clean. Let the cakes cool for 15 minutes, then remove from the pans and cool completely on a wire rack.

To assemble the cake: Level the top of one of the cake layers with a serrated knife so it is flat. Place the layer cut side down on a serving plate (you can keep the edges of the plate clean by sliding strips of parchment underneath the cake while you frost it). Using an offset spatula, spread the top of the layer with a big dollop of frosting. Place the second layer on top, right side up, and frost the top and sides with the remaining frosting, making big swirls with the spatula or a butter knife.

The cake can be stored wrapped in plastic wrap in the refrigerator for up to 3 days.

continued

Cream Cheese Frosting

MAKES ABOUT 5 CUPS

8 TABLESPOONS (1 STICK) UNSALTED
BUTTER, CUT INTO CHUNKS,
AT ROOM TEMPERATURE

TWO 8-OUNCE PACKAGES CREAM
CHEESE, CUT INTO CHUNKS,
AT ROOM TEMPERATURE

1 TABLESPOON PURE
VANILLA EXTRACT

5 TO 6 CUPS CONFECTIONERS'
SUGAR

In the bowl of a stand mixer fitted with the paddle attachment (or in a large mixing bowl, using a handheld mixer), beat the butter, cream cheese, and vanilla until smooth and creamy, 3 to 5 minutes. Gradually add the confectioners' sugar, beating until light and fluffy, 5 to 7 minutes.

The frosting can be stored in an airtight container at room temperature for up to 2 days.

VARIATION

Spiced Cream Cheese Frosting: Add ½ teaspoon ground cinnamon when you add the confectioners' sugar.

HUMMINGBIRD CAKE WITH CREAM CHEESE FROSTING

SERVES 10 TO 12

Spiced with cinnamon and studded with pecans, this cake is a true Southern classic. Bananas and pineapple give it a luscious texture, and its flavors mingle and grow more intense the day after it's baked.

3 CUPS UNBLEACHED ALL-PURPOSE FLOUR

1 TEASPOON BAKING SODA

1 TEASPOON GROUND CINNAMON

½ TEASPOON GROUND MACE

1 TEASPOON FINE SEA SALT

1 CUP GRANULATED SUGAR

1 CUP PACKED LIGHT BROWN SUGAR

1¼ CUPS CANOLA OIL

3 LARGE EGGS

2 TEASPOONS PURE VANILLA EXTRACT

2 CUPS MASHED VERY RIPE BANANAS (ABOUT 5 LARGE BANANAS)

ONE 8-OUNCE CAN CRUSHED PINEAPPLE, DRAINED

1½ CUPS CHOPPED PECANS

1 RECIPE CREAM CHEESE FROSTING (OPPOSITE)

Position a rack in the lower third of the oven and preheat the oven to 350°F. Butter two 9-inch round cake pans, then line the bottoms with parchment and butter it as well. Lightly dust the pans with flour, tapping the pans on the counter to shake out the excess.

Sift together the flour, baking soda, cinnamon, mace, and salt; set aside.

In the bowl of a stand mixer fitted with the paddle attachment (or in a large mixing bowl, using a handheld mixer), beat both sugars with the oil for 2 to 3 minutes, until smooth. Add the eggs one at a time, beating well after each addition, then mix

for 2 minutes, until light and fluffy. Add the vanilla, bananas, and pineapple, mixing until just combined. On low speed, add the flour mixture in thirds, beating until combined; scrape down the sides of the bowl as necessary. Fold in ½ cup of the pecans.

Divide the batter evenly between the prepared pans and smooth the tops with a spatula. Tap the pans firmly on the counter to remove any air bubbles from the batter. Bake for 40 to 50 minutes, until a cake tester inserted in the center of a cake comes out clean. Let the cakes cool for 15 minutes, then remove the layers from the pans and cool completely on a wire rack.

To assemble the cake: Level the top of one of the cake layers with a serrated knife so it is flat. Place the layer cut side down on a serving plate (you can keep the edges of the plate clean by sliding strips of parchment underneath the cake while you frost it). Using an offset spatula or a butter knife, spread the top of the layer with a dollop of frosting. Place the second layer on top, right side up, and frost the top and sides with the remaining frosting. Decorate the sides of the cake with the remaining 1 cup pecans.

The cake can be stored wrapped in plastic wrap in the refrigerator for up to 3 days. Serve at room temperature.

CARROT CAKE WITH SPICED CREAM CHEESE FROSTING

SERVES 10 TO 12

This traditional dessert is studded with sweet black currants, spices, and pecans, giving a flavor profile that tastes even better the day after the cake is baked. The use of black currants was a happy accident that resulted when we ordered a large shipment of them instead of the dark raisins we wanted for the bakery. We decided to give them a try and loved the little sweet notes they add in this recipe.

2 CUPS UNBLEACHED
ALL-PURPOSE FLOUR

2 TEASPOONS BAKING POWDER,
PREFERABLY ALUMINUM-FREE

2 TEASPOONS BAKING SODA

2 TEASPOONS GROUND CINNAMON

½ TEASPOON FRESHLY GRATED
NUTMEG

1 TEASPOON FINE SEA SALT

1¼ CUPS CANOLA OIL

4 LARGE EGGS

1 CUP GRANULATED SUGAR

1 CUP PACKED LIGHT BROWN SUGAR

1 TEASPOON PURE VANILLA EXTRACT

4 CUPS FINELY GRATED CARROTS
(4 TO 5 LARGE CARROTS)

½ CUP DRIED CURRANTS

1 CUP CHOPPED PECANS

1 RECIPE SPICED CREAM CHEESE
FROSTING (SEE PAGE 28)

Position a rack in the lower third of the oven and preheat the oven to 350°F. Butter two 9-inch round cake pans. Line the bottoms with parchment and butter it as well. Lightly dust the pans with flour, tapping the pans on the counter to shake out the excess.

32

Sift together the flour, baking powder, baking soda, cinnamon, nutmeg, and salt; set aside.

In a large mixing bowl, combine the oil, eggs, both sugars, and vanilla and whisk until the mixture looks light and pale in color. Fold in the flour mixture in thirds until just combined. Gently fold in the carrots, currants, and ½ cup of the pecans until thoroughly combined.

Divide the batter evenly between the prepared pans and smooth the tops with a spatula. Tap the pans firmly on the counter to remove any air bubbles from the batter.

Bake for 40 to 50 minutes, until the center of a cake springs back a little when touched and a cake tester inserted in the center of a cake comes out clean. Let cool for 20 minutes, then remove the layers from the pans and transfer to a wire rack to cool completely.

To assemble the cake: Level the top of one of the cake layers with a serrated knife so it is flat. Place the layer cut side down on a serving plate (you can keep the edges of the plate clean by sliding strips of parchment underneath the cake while you frost it). Using an offset spatula, spread the top of the layer with a dollop of frosting. Place the second layer on top, right side up, and frost the top and sides with the remaining frosting. Decorate the top or sides of the cake with the remaining ½ cup pecans.

The cake can be stored wrapped in plastic wrap in the refrigerator for up to 2 days.

CAKETTE PARTY CAKE WITH ITALIAN MERINGUE BUTTERCREAM

SERVES 12 TO 16

This cake is a little bit fancy and looks like a party when you open the box. It is a delicate, light white cake, with a bit of buttermilk in the batter that gives it an extra-tender and moist crumb. The Italian meringue buttercream has a consistency similar to that of fluffy whipped cream and is not as sweet as frostings made with confectioners' sugar. The flavor options with this frosting are endless; add a few drops of your favorite extract or liqueur.

3 CUPS CAKE FLOUR (NOT SELF-RISING)

1½ TEASPOONS BAKING POWDER, PREFERABLY ALUMINUM-FREE

¾ TEASPOON BAKING SODA

¾ TEASPOON FINE SEA SALT

¾ POUND (3 STICKS) UNSALTED BUTTER, AT ROOM TEMPERATURE

2⅓ CUPS GRANULATED SUGAR

3 LARGE EGG WHITES

2 TEASPOONS PURE VANILLA EXTRACT

1½ CUPS BUTTERMILK

1 RECIPE ITALIAN MERINGUE BUTTERCREAM (RECIPE FOLLOWS)

Position a rack in the middle of the oven and preheat the oven to 350°F. Butter a baking sheet, then line it with parchment, leaving an overhang on the two short ends of the pan. Butter the parchment as well, and lightly dust with flour, tapping the pan on the counter to shake out the excess.

Sift together the flour, baking powder, baking soda, and salt. Set aside.

In the bowl of a stand mixer fitted with the paddle attachment (or in a

large mixing bowl, using a handheld mixer), cream the butter and sugar on medium-high speed for 3 to 5 minutes, until light and fluffy. Scrape down the sides of the bowl. Turn the mixer speed down to low, add the egg whites and vanilla, and mix until completely incorporated.

With the mixer on low speed, add the flour mixture in thirds, alternating with the buttermilk and beginning and ending with the flour, mixing until just combined.

Remove the bowl from the mixer and, using a rubber spatula, incorporate any ingredients hiding at the bottom of the bowl, making sure the batter is completely mixed. Pour the batter into the prepared pan and gently smooth the top with a spatula. Tap the pan firmly on the counter to remove any air bubbles from the batter.

Bake for 20 to 25 minutes, until a cake tester inserted in the center of the cake comes out clean and the cake is lightly golden. Let the cake cool for 15 minutes, then carefully remove it, using the parchment "handles" from the pan, to cool completely on a wire rack. Peel off the parchment.

To assemble the cake: Cut the cake in half and then in half again, making four pieces. Place the first piece upside down on a serving plate (you can keep the edges of the plate clean by sliding strips of parchment underneath the cake while you frost it). Using an offset spatula, spread the top of the layer with a big dollop of the buttercream (see Tip). Place the second layer upside down on the first layer and frost the top. Repeat with the third layer. Then put the final layer on top, upside down. Frost the top and sides of the cake with a thin layer of frosting—the crumb coat—and set in the refrigerator to chill for at least 30 minutes.

Remove the cake from the refrigerator and frost with the remaining frosting.

The cake is best served at room temperature, but it can be stored wrapped in plastic wrap in the refrigerator for up to 3 days.

TIP: I like to decorate my cakes by creating texture in the frosting using a spatula or a butter knife. Don't worry about getting the frosting perfectly smooth. Then decorate the top of the cake with edible fresh flowers, buttercream flowers, or paper flags. Have fun with it!

Italian Meringue Buttercream

MAKES 10 CUPS

2 CUPS GRANULATED SUGAR

10 LARGE EGG WHITES,
AT ROOM TEMPERATURE

1¼ TEASPOONS CREAM OF TARTAR

2 POUNDS UNSALTED BUTTER,
CUT INTO ½-INCH CHUNKS,
AT ROOM TEMPERATURE

1 TABLESPOON PURE
VANILLA EXTRACT

SPECIAL EQUIPMENT

CANDY THERMOMETER

In a small saucepan, combine 1½ cups of the sugar and ½ cup water and cook over medium heat, stirring occasionally, until the sugar has dissolved. Brush down the sides of the saucepan with a pastry brush dipped in warm water to remove any crystals, then do not stir again. Clip a candy thermometer to the side of the saucepan and cook until the syrup reaches 248°F (the "firm ball stage"), 8 to 10 minutes. Keep a constant eye on the thermometer.

Meanwhile, combine the egg whites and cream of tartar in the bowl of a stand mixer fitted with the whisk attachment (or use a large mixing bowl and a handheld mixer) and beat until the whites are foamy and barely hold soft peaks. Gradually add the remaining ½ cup sugar and then whisk for another 1 to 2 minutes, until the meringue holds soft peaks. Turn the mixer off.

As soon as the sugar syrup reaches 248°F, carefully lift the pan from the heat (use an oven mitt) and, with the mixer running on low, carefully pour the hot syrup into the egg white mixture in a slow, steady stream, avoiding the spinning whisk. Be careful: the syrup is very hot, and you don't want it to splash. Once all the syrup is added, raise the speed to high and beat until the meringue has cooled to room temperature, 8 to 12 minutes. It will have expanded greatly and will look like marshmallow cream. (The mixture will deflate as soon as you start adding butter.)

Once the mixture has cooled to room temperature, begin adding the butter. Switch to the paddle attachment if using a stand mixer and, beating on medium speed, drop in the butter a few chunks at a time, waiting for it to be incorporated each time before adding more and scraping down the sides of the bowl as needed. Don't worry if the mixture begins to look curdled; if that happens, slow down and make sure that you are completely incorporating the butter before adding more. When all of the butter has been incorporated, add the vanilla, raise the speed to high, and whip for 1 to 2 minutes. The buttercream should be smooth, thick, and glossy.

Use the buttercream immediately. Or store it in an airtight container in the refrigerator for up to 1 week. To use buttercream that has been chilled, see the Tip.

TIP: To use buttercream that has been chilled, remove it from the refrigerator and bring it to room temperature. Make sure that it is softened to room temperature before you use it; if the butter is too cold, the buttercream will break and be a hot mess! Transfer the buttercream to the bowl of a stand mixer fitted with the paddle attachment (or to a large bowl if using a handheld mixer) and beat on medium speed until soft and spreadable, 2 to 3 minutes.

VARIATIONS

You can add different flavors to customize the frosting. For each 1 cup buttercream, add 3 tablespoons Lemon Curd (see page 56) or raspberry jam and 1 tablespoon of your favorite liqueur, such as Grand Marnier, amaretto, or Chambord, and replace the vanilla with 1 tablespoon almond, mint, or coconut extract.

HOW TO MAKE A
TIERED CELEBRATION CAKE

MAKES ONE 6- OR 7-LAYER 2-TIER CELEBRATION CAKE; SERVES 25 TO 30

There is nothing like a handmade celebration cake baked from scratch. Whether it's for a birthday or a wedding, it is absolutely the best gift you can ever give. Back in the day, celebration cakes were baked by the best baker in the family (or a close family friend) and given as a gift to the bride and groom. Griff and I still carry on this tradition today, and our closest friends always appreciate the gesture. So much time, effort, and love go into making a tiered celebration cake. The secret? Plan well in advance so that you can stay ahead of the unexpected. Once all of the elements are made, you can have fun and leave only the decorating for the night before the party. It's as easy as 1, 2, 3, 4.

DAYS 1 AND 2

BAKE THE CAKE LAYERS AND MAKE THE SIMPLE SYRUP

DAY 3

MAKE THE BUTTERCREAM AND ASSEMBLE THE CAKE

DAY 4

DECORATE THE CAKE

WHAT YOU'LL NEED

2 RECIPES CAKETTE PARTY CAKE BATTER (SEE PAGE 34)

4 CUPS SIMPLE SYRUP (SEE PAGE 24)

2 RECIPES ITALIAN MERINGUE BUTTERCREAM (PAGE 37)

THREE 9-INCH AND THREE 6-INCH ROUND CAKE PANS

THREE 9-INCH AND THREE 6-INCH CARDBOARD CAKE ROUNDS (SEE RESOURCES, PAGE 105)

DECORATING TURNTABLE

ONE 10- OR 12-INCH CAKE STAND PLATE

4 PLASTIC DRINKING STRAWS

continued

To bake the cakes: Position the racks in the middle and lower third of the oven and preheat the oven to 350°F. Butter three 6-inch round cake pans and three 9-inch round cake pans. Line the bottoms with parchment and butter that as well. Lightly dust the pans with flour, tapping the pans on the counter to shake out the excess.

Pour the batter into the pans, using about 2 cups batter for each 6-inch pan and about 3 cups for each 9-inch pan. Smooth the tops and tap the pans on the counter to remove any air bubbles. Bake until the cakes are lightly golden and a cake tester inserted in the center of a cake comes out clean: the 6-inch cake layers need 20 to 25 minutes, and the 9-inch layers need 30 to 35 minutes. Let the cakes cool for 15 minutes, then remove from the pans, peel off the parchment, and cool completely on wire racks.

Double-wrap the cooled layers in plastic and label them with the date. The cakes can be kept at room temperature for up to 2 days or refrigerated for up to 3 days. You can also freeze them for up to a week; transfer them to the refrigerator the night before you are ready to assemble the cake.

To prepare the cake layers: Level the tops of all of the cake layers with a serrated knife. Put a dab of frosting on a 6-inch cardboard cake round (to anchor the cake) and put one of the small layers cut side down on the round, then put it on a decorating turntable. Brush the layer generously with simple syrup (about 2 tablespoons). Using an offset spatula or a butter knife, spread the layer with a big dollop of frosting. Place another 6-inch cake layer upside down on top and brush with syrup. Frost the top and sides with a thin layer of frosting (the crumb coat). Refrigerate for at least 1 hour, then repeat with the final layer. Repeat the same process with the 9-inch cake layers. Once the frosting is set, wrap the tiers in plastic wrap and refrigerate until ready to assemble the cake.

continued

To assemble the cake: Remove the 9-inch tier from the refrigerator. Using an offset spatula or a butter knife, apply another, thicker layer of frosting over the top and sides. Then decorate the tier, making big or small swirls with the spatula or butter knife to create texture. Return to the refrigerator to chill and repeat with the 6-inch tier. Return to the refrigerator to chill.

Remove the 9-inch tier from the refrigerator and put it on the cake stand (or plate). Insert a plastic straw vertically through the center of the tier, mark the straw with kitchen shears at the point where it is level with the top of the cake, and remove the straw. Using the shears, cut the straw at the marked point. Using the straw as a guide, cut 3 more straws to this length. Press a 6-inch cardboard round gently down on the cake to make an outline of where the top tier should go. Insert the 4 straws at regular intervals just inside the circle outline to support the top tier (and keep it level), spacing them evenly. Position the 6-inch tier on top of the straws. Step back to admire your work. You did it!

DAY 4
·············

Finish decorating the cake as desired and top it off with vintage toppers or edible fresh flowers.

CARAMEL CAKE WITH SALTED CARAMEL FROSTING

SERVES 12 TO 16

Caramel cake is a true Southern American classic. The base is a delicate butter cake that is covered in a caramel frosting; we make a salted caramel version. Ours has a bit of caramel in the cake batter too, which makes it even richer. The best part is that you can make this cake a day ahead of your party, because the flavors get even better with time.

2½ CUPS UNBLEACHED ALL-PURPOSE FLOUR

2½ TEASPOONS BAKING POWDER, PREFERABLY ALUMINUM-FREE

1 TEASPOON FINE SEA SALT

1 CUP SALTED CARAMEL SAUCE (RECIPE FOLLOWS)

1⅓ CUPS GRANULATED SUGAR

8 TABLESPOONS (1 STICK) UNSALTED BUTTER, AT ROOM TEMPERATURE

3 LARGE EGGS, AT ROOM TEMPERATURE

SALTED CARAMEL FROSTING (RECIPE FOLLOWS)

FLAKY SEA SALT, SUCH AS JACOBSEN OR MALDON, OR FLEUR DE SEL FOR SPRINKLING

Position a rack in the lower third of the oven and preheat the oven to 350°F. Butter two 9-inch round cake pans, line the bottoms with parchment, and butter it as well. Lightly dust the pans with flour, tapping the pans on the counter to shake out the excess.

Sift together the flour, baking powder, and fine sea salt. Set aside.

In a small bowl, combine the caramel sauce and ½ cup water and stir until completely smooth. Set aside.

continued

Party Cakes

In the bowl of a stand mixer fitted with the paddle attachment (or in a large mixing bowl, using a handheld mixer), cream the sugar and butter together on medium-high speed for 3 to 5 minutes, until light and fluffy. Add the eggs one at a time, beating well after each addition and scraping down the sides of the bowl with a rubber spatula as necessary.

With the mixer on low speed, add the flour mixture in thirds, alternating with the caramel mixture and beginning and ending with the flour, mixing just until combined. Scrape down the sides of the bowl with a rubber spatula as necessary.

Divide the batter evenly between the prepared pans and smooth the tops with a spatula.

Bake for 25 to 30 minutes, until a cake tester inserted in the center of a cake layer comes out clean. Let the cakes cool for 20 minutes, then remove from the pans, peel off the parchment, and cool completely on a wire rack.

To assemble the cake: Level the top of one of the cake layers with a serrated knife so it is flat. Place the layer cut side down on a serving plate (you can keep the edges of the plate clean by sliding strips of parchment underneath the cake while you frost it). Using an offset spatula or a butter knife, spread the top of the layer with a big dollop of frosting. Place the second layer on top, right side up, and frost the top and sides with the remaining frosting, making big swirls with the spatula or butter knife. Sprinkle a little flaky sea salt over the top of the cake.

The cake is best served at room temperature, but it can be stored wrapped in plastic wrap in the refrigerator for up to 3 days.

continued

Salted Caramel Sauce

MAKES ABOUT 1½ CUPS

How can something so simple be so good? Salted caramel sauce is just sugar, cream, salt, and your loving time. You will be tempted to lick the spoon, but wait until the sauce is just warm to the touch. Drizzle it over ice cream or use it for the Caramel Cake (page 43).

¾ CUP HEAVY CREAM

1 CUP GRANULATED SUGAR

¼ TEASPOON FLAKY SEA SALT, SUCH AS JACOBSEN OR MALDON (SEE TIP)

Pull the cream out of the refrigerator an hour or so in advance to come up to room temperature. Or heat it in a microwave-safe bowl for 30-second intervals until it is at room temperature, a minute or so. Set aside.

Put 2 tablespoons of the sugar in a heavy nonreactive saucepan and set over medium heat. Watch closely as the sugar melts around the edges and starts to turn a beautiful amber color: you are making caramel. Stir the sugar with a heat-resistant spoon, then add another 2 tablespoons sugar and cook it in the same way. Continue to add the rest of the sugar 2 tablespoons at a time, waiting for it to be completely melted each time before adding more and stirring frequently as it melts and the color deepens. Do not walk away even for a second—the sugar can go from golden caramel to burnt in a flash.

When the caramel is a deep mahogany color, remove the pan from the heat and immediately, but slowly, pour in the cream. (If the cream is cold, the caramel will seize up and you may get some lumps of hardened caramel, but if this happens, there is no need to panic—just return the pan to the stove and stir over low heat until the

caramel is completely melted and smooth.) Stir in the sea salt and let cool.

The sauce can be stored in an airtight container in the refrigerator for up to 2 weeks. When you are ready to use it, place the container in a large bowl of hot water and gently stir until it warms up and is ready to drizzle.

TIP: At the bakery, we invest in pure sea salts to give the final flourish to some of our baked goods and savory dishes too. One of our favorites, Jacobsen Salt Co. sea salt, is hand-harvested off the Oregon coast. The salt is flaky and delicious, and a small pinch makes a world of difference for brownies, cookies, popcorn, and, of course, the salted caramel sauce.

Salted Caramel Frosting

MAKES ABOUT 5 CUPS

2 CUPS PACKED DARK BROWN SUGAR

12 TABLESPOONS (1½ STICKS) UNSALTED BUTTER, CUT INTO TABLESPOON-SIZED PIECES

½ TEASPOON FINE SEA SALT

½ CUP HEAVY CREAM

1½ TEASPOONS PURE VANILLA EXTRACT

2½ CUPS CONFECTIONERS' SUGAR, SIFTED

In a heavy saucepan, combine the brown sugar, 8 tablespoons (1 stick) of the butter, and the salt and cook over medium heat, stirring constantly, until the mixture comes to a gentle boil, 5 to 8 minutes. Whisk in the cream and continue to cook until it comes to a boil again. Take off the heat and add the vanilla.

Pour the mixture into the bowl of a stand mixer fitted with the paddle attachment (or use a large mixing bowl and a handheld mixer) and, with the mixer on low speed, gradually add the confectioners' sugar, beating until incorporated. Turn the mixer up to medium speed and beat until the frosting is a pale brown and cooled to warm, 3 to 5 minutes. Add the remaining 4 tablespoons butter a little at a time and continue to mix until light and fluffy.

Use the frosting immediately.

TIP: When decorating cakes, I always take the time to apply a thin layer of frosting, called a "crumb coat," first and then refrigerate the cake for at least 30 minutes (or as long as overnight). This simple step traps any loose crumbs in that first layer of frosting so that the final layer of frosting will be smooth. It also keeps the cake in place (so you don't have a tipsy-topsy cake!). Put a bit of your frosting in a separate bowl for the crumb coat to keep the larger batch of frosting crumb-free. Then check the cake after it has set for about 10 minutes to make sure that it hasn't shifted. You can adjust it if necessary before the frosting has completely set.

CHOCOLATE CREAM CAKE WITH DARK CHOCOLATE GANACHE

SERVES 12 TO 16

The coffee in this chocolate cake batter really makes the flavor sing.

2⅓ CUPS CAKE FLOUR (NOT SELF-RISING)

1 CUP DUTCH-PROCESSED COCOA POWDER

¼ TEASPOON BAKING POWDER, PREFERABLY ALUMINUM-FREE

1½ TEASPOONS BAKING SODA

1 TEASPOON FINE SEA SALT

1 CUP HOT STRONG COFFEE

1 CUP BUTTERMILK

½ POUND (2 STICKS) UNSALTED BUTTER, AT ROOM TEMPERATURE

2½ CUPS GRANULATED SUGAR

4 LARGE EGGS, AT ROOM TEMPERATURE

1 LARGE EGG YOLK, AT ROOM TEMPERATURE

2 TEASPOONS PURE VANILLA EXTRACT

¼ POUND SEMISWEET CHOCOLATE, MELTED AND SLIGHTLY COOLED

½ CUP SIMPLE SYRUP (SEE PAGE 24)

1 RECIPE WHIPPED BUTTERCREAM FROSTING (RECIPE FOLLOWS)

1 RECIPE DARK CHOCOLATE GANACHE (RECIPE FOLLOWS)

Position a rack in the middle of the oven and preheat the oven to 350°F. Butter three 9-inch round cake pans, then line the bottoms with parchment and butter it as well. Lightly dust the pans with flour, tapping the pans on the counter to shake out the excess.

Sift together the flour, cocoa, baking powder, baking soda, and salt. Set aside.

In a small bowl, whisk the hot coffee and buttermilk together. Set aside.

continued

In the bowl of a stand mixer fitted with the paddle attachment (or in a large mixing bowl, using a handheld mixer), cream the butter and sugar on medium-high speed for 3 to 5 minutes, until light and fluffy. Turn the mixer speed down to low and add the eggs and yolk one at a time, mixing well after each addition. Add the vanilla and mix until combined. Then mix on high speed until the batter is doubled in volume and very light and fluffy, about 3 minutes. Scrape down the sides of the bowl with a rubber spatula and mix for another minute.

On low speed, add the flour mixture in thirds, alternating with the coffee and buttermilk mixture and beginning and ending with the flour, mixing until just combined. Beat in the melted chocolate.

Remove the bowl from the mixer and, using a rubber spatula, make sure the ingredients are well incorporated. Divide the batter evenly among the prepared pans and smooth the tops.

Bake for 25 to 30 minutes, until a cake tester inserted in the center of a cake comes out clean. Let the cakes cool for 20 minutes, then remove from the pans, peel off the parchment, and cool completely on a wire rack.

To assemble the cake: Level the tops of two of the cake layers with a serrated knife so they are flat. Place one layer cut side down on a serving plate. Generously brush some simple syrup on top of the cake layer. Using an offset spatula or a butter knife, spread the top of the layer with a dollop of frosting. Place the second cake layer cut side down on top and repeat. Place the final cake layer right side up on top and frost the top with another big dollop of frosting. Place the cake in the refrigerator for at least 1 hour, or overnight, to set the frosting.

Using an offset spatula or a butter knife, frost the top and sides of the cake with the ganache. Finish decorating by making big swirls with the spatula or butter knife.

The cake can be stored wrapped in plastic wrap in the refrigerator for up to 3 days.

Whipped Buttercream Frosting

MAKES 3½ CUPS

¼ CUP UNBLEACHED
ALL-PURPOSE FLOUR

1 CUP WHOLE MILK

½ POUND (2 STICKS) UNSALTED
BUTTER, AT ROOM TEMPERATURE

1 TEASPOON PURE VANILLA EXTRACT

1 CUP GRANULATED SUGAR

Combine the flour and ¼ cup of the milk in a small heavy saucepan and whisk until blended. Set the pan over medium heat and gradually add the remaining ¾ cup milk, whisking constantly, then cook, whisking, until the mixture comes to a low boil. Reduce the heat to low and whisk until the mixture begins to thicken and starts to "burp," 2 to 3 minutes.

Transfer the mixture to a small heatproof bowl and stir occasionally as it cools to keep it lump-free. If you do get a few lumps, don't worry—you can whisk the mixture to dissolve the lumps, or pass it through a fine-mesh sieve. (You can put the mixture in the refrigerator for 10 minutes to speed up the cooling process.)

In the bowl of a stand mixer fitted with the whisk attachment (or in a large bowl, using a handheld mixer), whip the butter and vanilla on medium speed until soft and creamy, 2 to 3 minutes. Gradually add the sugar and then beat on high speed until the mixture is light and fluffy, 5 to 7 minutes.

Reduce the speed to low and gradually add the milk mixture, then increase the speed to medium-high and whip until the frosting is light and fluffy, scraping down the sides of the bowl with a rubber spatula as necessary.

Use the frosting immediately. Or store in an airtight container in the refrigerator for up to 2 days. To use buttercream that has been chilled, see the Tip on page 38.

Party Cakes

Dark Chocolate Ganache

MAKES ABOUT 3 CUPS

1 CUP HEAVY CREAM

8 TABLESPOONS (1 STICK) UNSALTED BUTTER, CUT INTO 1-INCH PIECES

⅓ CUP GRANULATED SUGAR

¼ TEASPOON FINE SEA SALT

1 POUND SEMISWEET CHOCOLATE, FINELY CHOPPED

¼ CUP HOT COFFEE

1 TEASPOON PURE VANILLA EXTRACT

Combine the cream, butter, sugar, and salt in a heatproof bowl, set it over a saucepan of simmering water (do not let the bottom of the bowl touch the water), and stir occasionally until the butter is melted. Add the chocolate and stir until it is completely melted and the mixture is smooth.

Take off the heat and stir in the coffee and vanilla until smooth, then stir occasionally as the ganache cools and thickens. Making the perfect ganache cannot be rushed: resist the urge to refrigerate it or whisk it to cool it faster. Once it is thickened and glistening, you are ready to frost your cake.

JANIE Q'S LEMON CAKE WITH LEMON MERINGUE BUTTERCREAM

SERVES 12 TO 16

My mom was the queen of lemon meringue pie. (Her name was really Janie Queen!) I created this cake in her honor; I wanted to convey her happy personality in cake form. It's a light and delicate cake filled with a fresh bright lemon curd and covered in a luscious lemon meringue buttercream. You will taste a bit of sunshine in every bite.

2½ CUPS CAKE FLOUR
(NOT SELF-RISING)

2½ TEASPOONS BAKING POWDER,
PREFERABLY ALUMINUM-FREE

1 TEASPOON FINE SEA SALT

½ CUP WHOLE MILK

1 TEASPOON PURE VANILLA EXTRACT

½ POUND (2 STICKS) UNSALTED
BUTTER, AT ROOM TEMPERATURE

1½ CUPS GRANULATED SUGAR

2 TABLESPOONS GRATED LEMON ZEST

2 TABLESPOONS FRESH LEMON JUICE

4 LARGE EGGS,
AT ROOM TEMPERATURE

FOR THE LEMON CURD

7 LARGE EGG YOLKS

1 CUP GRANULATED SUGAR

½ CUP FRESH LEMON JUICE

4 TABLESPOONS COLD UNSALTED
BUTTER, CUBED

1 TABLESPOON GRATED LEMON ZEST

½ CUP VANILLA SIMPLE SYRUP
(SEE PAGE 24)

1 RECIPE LEMON MERINGUE
BUTTERCREAM (RECIPE FOLLOWS)

LEMON SLICES FOR DECORATION
(OPTIONAL)

Position a rack in the middle of the oven and preheat the oven to 350°F. Butter two 9-inch round cake pans, then line the bottoms with parchment and butter it as well. Lightly dust the pans with flour, tapping the pans on the counter to shake out the excess.

Sift together the flour, baking powder, and salt. Set aside.

In a measuring cup or a small bowl, whisk the milk and vanilla together. Set aside.

In the bowl of a stand mixer fitted with the paddle attachment (or in a large mixing bowl, using a handheld mixer), cream the butter and sugar with the lemon zest for 3 to 5 minutes, until light and fluffy. Beat in the lemon juice. Turn the mixer speed down to low and add the eggs one at a time, beating well after each addition and scraping down the sides of the bowl with a rubber spatula as necessary.

On low speed, add the flour mixture in thirds, alternating with the milk and vanilla and beginning and ending with the flour, mixing until just combined. Remove the bowl from the mixer and, using a rubber spatula, incorporate any ingredients hiding at the bottom of the bowl, making sure the batter is completely mixed.

Divide the batter evenly between the prepared pans and gently smooth the tops with a spatula. Tap the pans firmly on the counter to remove any air bubbles from the batter.

Bake for 25 to 35 minutes, until a cake tester inserted in the center of a cake comes out clean. Let the cakes cool for 15 minutes, then remove from the pans, peel off the parchment, and cool completely on a wire rack.

To make the lemon curd: Whisk the egg yolks, sugar, and lemon juice together in a heatproof bowl. Set the bowl over a medium saucepan of simmering water (do not let the bottom of the bowl touch the water) and cook, whisking frequently, until the mixture is thick and glossy, 8 to 10 minutes.

continued

Remove the curd from the heat and strain through a fine-mesh sieve into a bowl to make sure that there are no pesky bits of eggs remaining. Let the curd cool for about 10 minutes.

Whisk the butter into the curd. Fold in the lemon zest. Place a piece of plastic wrap directly on the surface of the curd so that a skin doesn't form, poke a few holes in the plastic to create steam vents, and let cool to room temperature.

Store the curd in an airtight container in the refrigerator for up to 1 week. You can also freeze it for up to 3 months.

To assemble the cake: Level the top of one of the cake layers with a serrated knife so it is flat. Place the layer cut side up on a serving plate (you can keep the edges of the plate clean by sliding strips of parchment underneath the cake while you frost it). Generously brush simple syrup on top of the cake layer.

Fit a pastry bag with a large plain tip (or use a large ziplock bag, with a bottom corner snipped off) and fill the bag halfway with the buttercream. Chill the remaining buttercream. Pipe a circle on the border of the layer to create a dam. Using an offset spatula or a butter knife, spread a big dollop of lemon curd in the middle of the frosting dam. Place the second layer on top, right side up, and frost the top and sides with a thin layer of frosting (the crumb coat). Place the cake in the refrigerator for at least 1 hour, or overnight, to set the frosting.

Using an offset spatula or a butter knife, frost the top and sides of the cake with the remaining buttercream. Finish by making big swirls with the spatula or butter knife. Decorate with lemon slices, if desired.

The cake can be stored wrapped in plastic wrap in the refrigerator for up to 3 days. Bring to room temperature before serving.

continued

Lemon Meringue Buttercream

6 LARGE EGG WHITES

1½ CUPS GRANULATED SUGAR

¼ TEASPOON FINE SEA SALT

1¼ POUNDS (5 STICKS) BUTTER,
CUT INTO ½-INCH CHUNKS,
AT ROOM TEMPERATURE

1½ TABLESPOONS GRATED LEMON ZEST

2 TABLESPOONS FRESH LEMON JUICE

OPTIONAL SPECIAL EQUIPMENT

CANDY OR INSTANT-READ THERMOMETER

In the bowl of a stand mixer (or in a large heatproof bowl), whisk the egg whites, sugar, and salt together. Set the bowl over a saucepan of simmering water (do not let the bottom of the bowl touch the water) and cook, whisking constantly, until the sugar is dissolved. The mixture will be warm to the touch and register 140°F on a candy or instant-read thermometer.

Remove the bowl from the heat, attach it to the mixer stand, and fit with the whisk attachment (or use a handheld mixer). Beat on high speed until stiff peaks form and the meringue cools to room temperature, 3 to 5 minutes.

Once the mixture has cooled to room temperature, replace the whisk with the paddle attachment and begin adding the butter a few chunks at a time, waiting for it to be incorporated before adding more and scraping down the sides of the bowl as needed. Don't worry if the mixture begins to look curdled; if that happens, slow down and make sure you are completely incorporating the butter before adding more. When all of the butter has been added, add the lemon zest and lemon juice and beat for another 1 to 2 minutes. The frosting should be smooth, thick, and glossy.

Use the buttercream immediately. Or store it in an airtight container in the refrigerator for up to 1 week. To use buttercream that has been chilled, see the Tip on page 38.

ALABAMA LANE CAKE

SERVES 12 TO 16

Lane Cake is mentioned several times in one of my all-time favorite novels, *To Kill a Mockingbird*; it even stirs up a rivalry between two of the neighborhood home bakers. This old-timey cake, which is also known as Prize Cake, was created by Emma Rylander Lane of Alabama, who won first prize with it at the county fair in Columbus, Georgia, at the turn of the twentieth century. It's a moist white cake filled and frosted with a whiskey-laced custard, coconut, dried fruit, and pecans. The flavors are even better the next day (and the day after that). Lane Cake has been a tradition in my family for generations. We always serve it for celebrations and especially at Christmastime, and it has memories built into every slice.

3½ CUPS CAKE FLOUR (NOT SELF-RISING)

1 TABLESPOON BAKING POWDER, PREFERABLY ALUMINUM-FREE

¼ TEASPOON FINE SEA SALT

1 CUP WHOLE MILK

1 TEASPOON PURE VANILLA EXTRACT

½ POUND (2 STICKS) UNSALTED BUTTER, AT ROOM TEMPERATURE

2 CUPS GRANULATED SUGAR

8 LARGE EGG WHITES

FOR THE FROSTING

1½ CUPS PECANS

12 TABLESPOONS (1½ STICKS) UNSALTED BUTTER

1½ CUPS GRANULATED SUGAR

12 LARGE EGG YOLKS

1½ CUPS SWEETENED FLAKED COCONUT

1½ CUPS GOLDEN RAISINS, FINELY CHOPPED

½ CUP BOURBON OR BRANDY

OPTIONAL SPECIAL EQUIPMENT

INSTANT-READ THERMOMETER

continued

Position a rack in the middle of the oven and preheat the oven to 350°F. Butter three 9-inch round cake pans, line the bottoms with parchment, and butter it as well. Lightly dust the pans with flour, tapping the pans on the counter to shake out the excess.

Sift together the flour, baking powder, and salt. Set aside.

In a measuring cup or a small bowl, combine the milk and vanilla. Set aside.

In the bowl of a stand mixer fitted with the paddle attachment (or in a large mixing bowl, using a handheld mixer), cream the butter and sugar on medium-high speed for 3 to 5 minutes, until light and fluffy. Turn the mixer speed down to low and add the flour mixture in thirds, alternating with the milk and beginning and ending with the flour, mixing just until combined; scrape down the sides of the bowl with a rubber spatula as necessary. If using a stand mixer, transfer to another large bowl.

In the very clean mixer bowl (or in another large bowl), using the clean whisk (or clean beaters), beat the egg whites until they hold soft peaks. Fold one-quarter of the egg whites into the cake batter to lighten it, then gently fold in the remaining egg whites until incorporated.

Divide the batter evenly among the prepared pans and smooth the tops with a spatula. Bake for 25 to 30 minutes, until a cake tester inserted in the center of a cake comes out clean. Let the cake cool for 15 minutes, then remove from the pans, peel off the parchment, and cool completely on a wire rack.

Preheat the oven to 350°F.

To make the frosting: Spread the pecans on a baking sheet and toast in the oven for 6 to 8 minutes. Set aside to cool, then finely chop.

In a medium saucepan, melt the butter. Remove from the heat and let cool to tepid, then whisk in the sugar and egg yolks until smooth.

continued

Set the pan over medium heat and cook, stirring constantly with a wooden spoon, until the filling has thickened enough to coat the back of the spoon; it should read 180°F on an instant-read thermometer. Be careful not to let the mixture come to a boil.

Remove from the heat and add the toasted pecans, coconut, golden raisins, and bourbon, stirring well. Transfer the frosting to a heatproof bowl to cool; it will continue to thicken as it cools. It will be ooey and gooey, and that is exactly what you want.

To assemble the cake: Level the tops of two of the cake layers with a serrated knife so they are flat. Place one layer cut side down on a serving plate (you can keep the edges of the plate clean by sliding strips of parchment underneath the cake while you frost it). Using an offset spatula or a butter knife, spread the layer with one-third of the frosting. Place the second cake layer cut side down on top of the first and spread with another third of the frosting. Place the final layer right side up on top and frost the top with the remaining frosting.

The cake can be stored at room temperature for up to 2 days or refrigerated for 4 days. Serve at room temperature.

BROWN SUGAR BUNDT CAKE WITH BUTTERSCOTCH GLAZE

I love the rolling mounds of this fluted Bundt cake, which allow the glossy butterscotch glaze to run lavishly down its sides. The glaze gives a smooth finish that is a wonderful complement to the cake's finely textured crumb. It is perfect at a Sunday brunch.

2¼ CUPS UNBLEACHED ALL-PURPOSE FLOUR

½ TEASPOON BAKING SODA

½ TEASPOON FINE SEA SALT

½ TEASPOON GROUND CARDAMOM

½ POUND (2 STICKS) UNSALTED BUTTER, AT ROOM TEMPERATURE

2 CUPS PACKED LIGHT BROWN SUGAR

1 TEASPOON PURE VANILLA EXTRACT

1 TEASPOON GRATED LEMON ZEST

3 LARGE EGGS, AT ROOM TEMPERATURE

1 CUP SOUR CREAM

FOR THE BUTTERSCOTCH GLAZE

7 TABLESPOONS UNSALTED BUTTER

1 CUP PACKED LIGHT BROWN SUGAR

1 CUP HEAVY CREAM

Position a rack in the lower third of the oven and preheat the oven to 325°F. Butter a 10-inch Bundt pan, making sure to get into the tight crevices. Lightly dust the pan with flour, tapping the pan on the counter to shake out the excess.

Sift together the flour, baking soda, salt, and cardamom; set aside.

continued

In the bowl of a stand mixer fitted with the paddle attachment (or in a large mixing bowl, using a handheld mixer), cream the butter and brown sugar on low to medium speed for 5 to 7 minutes, until light and fluffy. Add the vanilla and lemon zest and mix just to combine. Add the eggs one at a time, beating well after each addition. Add the flour mixture in thirds, alternating with the sour cream, beginning and ending with the flour, and mix for another 1 to 2 minutes.

Remove the bowl from the mixer and, using a rubber spatula, incorporate any ingredients hiding at the bottom of the bowl, making sure the batter is completely mixed. Pour the batter into the prepared pan. Tap the pan firmly on the counter to remove any air bubbles from the batter.

Bake for 60 to 75 minutes, until a cake tester inserted in the center of the cake comes out clean. Cool for 15 minutes, then remove from the pan and transfer to a wire rack to cool completely.

To make the butterscotch glaze: Put the butter, brown sugar, and cream in a medium saucepan and stir over medium heat until the sugar has completely dissolved. Bring to a boil and cook until thickened, about 5 minutes. Let the glaze cool slightly, then pour over the cooled cake.

The cake can be stored in an airtight container at room temperature for up to 2 days.

DEEP, DARK FLOURLESS CHOCOLATE CAKE

SERVES 8 TO 10

Your family and friends will ooh and aah when you treat them to this decadent dessert. The intensity of the chocolate flavor and the simplicity of the recipe make it a winner every time. Serve the cake warm with a dusting of confectioners' sugar or a scoop of vanilla ice cream.

8 TABLESPOONS (1 STICK) UNSALTED BUTTER, CUT INTO 1-INCH PIECES

8 OUNCES SEMISWEET CHOCOLATE, FINELY CHOPPED

1 TEASPOON PURE VANILLA EXTRACT

1 TEASPOON HOT FRESHLY BREWED COFFEE

2 TABLESPOONS GRAND MARNIER

1 TEASPOON GROUND CINNAMON

6 LARGE EGGS, SEPARATED

½ CUP GRANULATED SUGAR

CONFECTIONERS' SUGAR FOR DUSTING

Position a rack in the middle of the oven and preheat the oven to 350°F. Butter a 9-inch springform pan and lightly dust with granulated sugar, tapping the pan on the counter to shake out the excess.

Put the butter and chocolate in a heatproof bowl, set it over a pot of gently simmering water (do not let the bottom of the bowl touch the water), and stir occasionally until melted and smooth. Remove from the heat and stir in the vanilla, coffee, Grand Marnier, and cinnamon. Set aside to cool to room temperature.

In the bowl of a stand mixer fitted with the whisk attachment (or in a medium mixing bowl, using a handheld mixer), beat the egg yolks and granulated sugar together on high speed for 3 to 4 minutes, until pale yellow and thick; the mixture should be thick enough to form ribbons when the whisk is lifted. Gently fold one-quarter of the egg yolk mixture into the chocolate mixture, then add the chocolate-egg mixture to the remaining yolks and gently fold to combine.

In a clean mixing bowl or other large bowl, using a clean whisk (or clean beaters), beat the egg whites until they form soft peaks. Fold one-quarter of the egg whites into the chocolate mixture to lighten it, then gently fold in the remaining whites until just incorporated, being careful not to deflate the egg whites. It is better to have some traces of egg white than to overmix the batter and end up with a tough cake.

Wrap the sides and bottom of the prepared springform pan in heavy-duty aluminum foil and place the pan in a deep baking pan large enough to hold it. Pour the batter into the springform pan and spread evenly with a spatula. Fill the baking pan with enough hot water to come about halfway up the sides of the springform pan.

Bake for 30 to 35 minutes, until the cake is firm at the edges but still jiggles slightly in the center; it will set completely as it cools. Remove the pan from the water bath and cool the cake on a wire rack for about 10 minutes.

Gently run a knife around the edges of the pan to loosen the cake, then release the springform ring and remove it. Carefully transfer the cake to a serving plate. Slice and serve immediately, dusting each serving with confectioners' sugar.

SPICE CAKE
WITH BUTTERSCOTCH ICING

SERVES 12 TO 16

This is a delicious old-timey recipe inspired by our mentor, Jane Thompson. Jane used to own Mondo Bakery in Atlanta, and her spice cake was one of the first recipes she shared with us. It's an applesauce cake, made with lots of spices, cocoa powder, apricots, and walnuts, and it is absolutely delicious. Make it a part of your Thanksgiving dinner menu.

4 CUPS UNBLEACHED
ALL-PURPOSE FLOUR

¼ CUP UNSWEETENED
COCOA POWDER

1 TABLESPOON BAKING SODA

1½ TEASPOONS FINE SEA SALT

1 TEASPOON GROUND CINNAMON

1 TEASPOON GROUND CLOVES

1 TEASPOON FRESHLY
GRATED NUTMEG

1 TEASPOON GROUND ALLSPICE

½ POUND (2 STICKS) UNSALTED
BUTTER, AT ROOM TEMPERATURE

3 CUPS GRANULATED SUGAR

4 LARGE EGGS, AT ROOM TEMPERATURE

3 CUPS APPLESAUCE

1½ CUPS WALNUTS,
COARSELY CHOPPED

1½ CUPS DRIED APRICOTS,
COARSELY CHOPPED

1 RECIPE BUTTERSCOTCH ICING
(RECIPE FOLLOWS)

Position a rack in the middle of the oven and preheat the oven to 350°F. Spray a 10-inch Bundt pan with nonstick spray, making sure to get into all the crevices.

Sift together the flour, cocoa powder, baking soda, salt, cinnamon, cloves, nutmeg, and allspice. Set aside.

continued

In the bowl of a stand mixer fitted with the paddle attachment (or in a large mixing bowl, using a handheld mixer), cream the butter and sugar together on medium-high speed for 4 to 5 minutes, until light and fluffy. Add the eggs one at a time, mixing well after each addition and scraping down the sides of the bowl with a rubber spatula as necessary.

With the mixer on low speed, add the sifted dry ingredients in thirds, alternating with the applesauce and beginning and ending with the flour.

Remove the bowl from the mixer and gently fold in the walnuts and apricots. Scrape the batter into the prepared pan and spread it evenly with a spatula.

Bake for 50 to 60 minutes, until a cake tester inserted in the center of the cake comes out clean. Let the cake cool in the pan on a wire rack for 20 minutes, then invert it onto the rack and cool completely.

Once the cake has cooled, transfer it to a serving plate. Frost the top of the cake with the icing, letting it drip down the sides of the cake too so that everyone gets plenty of frosting in every bite.

The cake can be stored in an airtight container at room temperature for up to 5 days. It will get better every day as the spices make one happy marriage.

Butterscotch Icing

8 TABLESPOONS (1 STICK)
UNSALTED BUTTER

⅔ CUP PACKED DARK BROWN SUGAR

½ CUP HEAVY CREAM

3 CUPS CONFECTIONERS' SUGAR

1 TEASPOON PURE VANILLA EXTRACT

In a medium saucepan, melt the butter over medium heat. Add the brown sugar and whisk until the sugar has completely dissolved, about 3 minutes. Gradually add the cream, then continue whisking until smooth, 2 to 3 minutes. Transfer to the bowl of a stand mixer (or to a large bowl if using a handheld mixer) and let cool for 10 to 15 minutes, stirring occasionally.

Using the paddle attachment (or handheld mixer), mixing on medium speed, gradually add the confectioners' sugar and vanilla, then continue beating until the icing is slightly lighter in color and light and creamy in texture. Use immediately.

MEXICAN SPICE CAKE WITH CHOCOLATE GLAZE

SERVES 12 TO 16

Griff and I make up new recipes all the time: we might take inspiration from a savory meal at a restaurant, from a new spice, or from our travels. While there is no beer in this cake, we came up with the recipe after trying the sought-after Mexican Cake Beer made by Westbrook Brewing Company, just outside Charleston, South Carolina. It's an imperial stout beer aged with cocoa nibs, vanilla beans, cinnamon sticks, and chile peppers, which are all flavors in this cake.

¼ CUP HOT WATER

⅓ CUP DUTCH-PROCESSED COCOA POWDER

3 LARGE EGGS

1½ TEASPOONS PURE VANILLA EXTRACT

¾ CUP PLUS 2 TABLESPOONS UNBLEACHED ALL-PURPOSE FLOUR

1 TEASPOON BAKING POWDER, PREFERABLY ALUMINUM-FREE

½ TEASPOON GROUND CINNAMON

¼ TEASPOON CAYENNE PEPPER

PINCH OF FINE SEA SALT

12 TABLESPOONS (1½ STICKS) UNSALTED BUTTER, AT ROOM TEMPERATURE

1 CUP GRANULATED SUGAR

10 OUNCES (1⅔ CUPS) BITTERSWEET CHOCOLATE CHUNKS

2 TABLESPOONS COCOA NIBS

FOR THE CHOCOLATE GLAZE

¼ CUP HEAVY CREAM

4 TABLESPOONS UNSALTED BUTTER, CUT INTO CUBES

2 TABLESPOONS GRANULATED SUGAR

PINCH OF FINE SEA SALT

4 OUNCES BITTERSWEET CHOCOLATE, FINELY CHOPPED

½ TEASPOON PURE VANILLA EXTRACT

Position a rack in the middle of the oven and preheat the oven to 350°F. Spray a 9-inch square cake pan with nonstick spray. Lightly dust the pan with flour, tapping the pan on the counter to shake out the excess.

In a small mixing bowl, stir together the hot water and cocoa powder to make a stiff paste. Add the eggs and vanilla and stir until combined; the mixture will look a bit lumpy. Set aside.

In another small bowl, whisk the flour, baking powder, cinnamon, cayenne, and salt together. Set aside.

In the bowl of a stand mixer fitted with the paddle attachment (or in a large mixing bowl, using a handheld mixer), cream the butter and sugar on medium-high speed for 3 to 5 minutes, until light and fluffy. Turn the mixer speed down to low and add the flour mixture in thirds, beating well after each addition and scraping down the sides of the bowl with a rubber spatula as necessary. Add the cocoa mixture and mix on medium-high for another minute to lighten the batter.

Remove the bowl from the mixer and, using a rubber spatula, fold in the chocolate chunks and cocoa nibs. Pour the batter into the prepared pan.

Bake for 40 to 45 minutes, until a cake tester inserted in the center of the cake comes out clean. Let the cake cool in the pan on a wire rack for 20 minutes, then invert onto the rack, turn right side up, and let cool completely.

To make the chocolate glaze: In a large heatproof bowl, combine the cream, butter, sugar, and salt, set over a saucepan of barely simmering water (do not let the bottom of the bowl touch the water), and stir until the butter is melted. Add the chocolate and stir until the chocolate has melted and the mixture is completely smooth. Remove from the heat. Stir in the vanilla.

Transfer the cake to a serving plate. Pour the chocolate glaze over the cake, letting it run down the sides. Let the glaze set before slicing and serving the cake.

The cake can be stored in an airtight container at room temperature for up to 3 days.

ANGEL FOOD CAKE WITH WHIPPED CREAM AND BERRIES

SERVES 12 TO 16

I will admit, angel food cake is second only to chocolate cake in my affections. I adore the delicate texture of the cake crumb, and I like to top slices with fresh summer berries and slather them with sweetened whipped cream—heaven on a plate. The egg whites are the key to making an angel food cake. To separate your eggs cleanly, do it when they are cold. Then let the whites come up to room temperature before you start. The yolks can go back into the fridge for another use (but be sure to use them within two days).

1⅓ CUPS CAKE FLOUR
(NOT SELF-RISING)

2 CUPS SUPERFINE SUGAR

½ TEASPOON FINE SEA SALT

1½ CUPS EGG WHITES (ABOUT 12),
AT ROOM TEMPERATURE

1 TEASPOON CREAM OF TARTAR

2 TEASPOONS PURE
VANILLA EXTRACT

1 RECIPE FRESH WHIPPED CREAM
(RECIPE FOLLOWS)

FRESH BERRIES FOR GARNISH

Position a rack in the lower third of the oven and preheat the oven to 350°F.

Using a sifter or a fine-mesh sieve, sift the flour, ½ cup of the sugar, and the salt together three times. Set aside.

In the impeccably clean bowl of a stand mixer fitted with the whisk attachment (or in a large mixing bowl, using a handheld mixer), beat

the egg whites and cream of tartar on medium speed until frothy, about 2 minutes. Add the remaining 1½ cups sugar 1 tablespoon at a time, beating on high speed, then beat until the egg whites are stiff and shiny. Add the vanilla and whip just until combined. Remove the bowl from the mixer.

Gently but thoroughly fold the flour mixture about one-quarter at a time into the egg whites. Spoon the batter into an ungreased 10-inch tube pan. (Don't be tempted to smack the pan against the kitchen counter to level the batter; you want to retain all of that air you just incorporated into your egg whites.)

Bake the cake for 35 to 40 minutes, until it is golden brown and a cake tester inserted in the center comes out clean. Invert the cake pan onto its feet onto the counter. If the pan does not have feet, invert it over a long-necked bottle, such as a wine bottle. (Cooling the cake upside down prevents it from deflating.) Let cool completely, about 1 hour.

Run a knife around the edges of the pan and the center tube to release the cake with ease and put it top side up on a serving plate. Serve with the whipped cream, garnished with berries.

The cake can be stored in an airtight container at room temperature for up to 3 days.

Fresh Whipped Cream

MAKES ABOUT 3 CUPS

2 CUPS HEAVY CREAM

¼ CUP CONFECTIONERS' SUGAR

In the bowl of a stand mixer fitted with the whisk attachment (or in a large mixing bowl, using a handheld mixer), whip the cream on medium speed until it starts to thicken. Add the confectioners' sugar and beat until the cream holds nice soft peaks.

Use the whipped cream immediately.

COCOA-COLA CAKE WITH CHOCOLATE ICING

SERVES 12 TO 16

This cake is full of chocolate goodness, inside and out, and both the cake and the frosting get a good dose of Coca-Cola. Be sure to use the real thing—diet soda will not work here! Mini marshmallows melt over the hot cake and are topped with chocolate icing and pecans.

Serve the kids the chocolaty cake with a glass of ice-cold milk; any day becomes a special occasion with this afternoon snack.

2 CUPS UNBLEACHED ALL-PURPOSE FLOUR

¼ CUP DUTCH-PROCESSED COCOA POWDER

1 TEASPOON BAKING SODA

1 CUP COCA-COLA, AT ROOM TEMPERATURE

½ CUP BUTTERMILK

2 TABLESPOONS PURE VANILLA EXTRACT

1¾ CUPS GRANULATED SUGAR

½ POUND (2 STICKS) UNSALTED BUTTER, AT ROOM TEMPERATURE

2 LARGE EGGS, AT ROOM TEMPERATURE

1½ CUPS MINI MARSHMALLOWS

FOR THE CHOCOLATE ICING

8 TABLESPOONS (1 STICK) UNSALTED BUTTER, MELTED

5 TABLESPOONS UNSWEETENED COCOA POWDER

⅓ CUP COCA-COLA

1 TEASPOON PURE VANILLA EXTRACT

ONE 16-OUNCE BOX CONFECTIONERS' SUGAR

1 CUP CHOPPED PECANS

Position a rack in the middle of the oven and preheat the oven to 350°F. Lightly spray a 9-by-13-inch baking pan with nonstick spray. Line with parchment, leaving an overhang on two opposite sides of the pan.

Sift together the flour, cocoa, and baking soda. Set aside.

In a small bowl, mix together the Coca-Cola, buttermilk, and vanilla. Set aside.

In the bowl of a stand mixer fitted with the paddle attachment (or in a large mixing bowl, using a handheld mixer), cream the sugar and butter on medium-high speed for 4 to 5 minutes, until light and fluffy. Add the eggs one at a time, mixing well after each addition and scraping down the sides of the bowl with a rubber spatula as necessary.

Turn the mixer speed down to low and add the flour mixture in thirds, alternating with the Coca-Cola mixture and beginning and ending with the flour. Remove the bowl from the mixer and, using the rubber spatula, incorporate any ingredients hiding at the bottom of the bowl, making sure the batter is completely mixed. Scrape the batter into the prepared pan and spread it evenly with a spatula.

Bake for 30 to 35 minutes, until a cake tester inserted in the center of the cake comes out clean. Scatter the marshmallows over the top of the hot cake and return to the oven for about 2 minutes, until they are melted.

In the meantime, make the chocolate icing: In a medium bowl, combine the melted butter, cocoa, Coca-Cola, and vanilla and mix with a spoon until smooth and creamy. Gradually add the confectioners' sugar, mixing until the icing is completely smooth. Fold in the pecans.

When the cake is done, remove from the oven and let cool on a wire rack for 10 minutes.

Spread the frosting over the warm cake. It will firm up as the cake cools.

The cake can be stored in an airtight container at room temperature for up to 3 days.

CLEMENTINE POUND CAKE WITH CHOCOLATE HONEY GLAZE

SERVES 8 TO 10

I love to bake with all types of citrus fruits in the winter, when apple season is over and berry season has yet to begin, and one of my favorites to bake with is the clementine. This cake is scented with clementine zest and the glaze is made with two different chocolates. The combination of orange and chocolate is a classic one, and there's a reason for that: the clementine's sweet tartness and the rich flavor of chocolate make a lovely pairing. Serve this as a satisfying after-dinner treat.

1½ CUPS CAKE FLOUR (NOT SELF-RISING)

½ TEASPOON BAKING POWDER, PREFERABLY ALUMINUM-FREE

¼ TEASPOON BAKING SODA

½ TEASPOON FINE SEA SALT

1¼ CUPS GRANULATED SUGAR

1 TABLESPOON GRATED CLEMENTINE ZEST

12 TABLESPOONS (1½ STICKS) UNSALTED BUTTER, AT ROOM TEMPERATURE

5 OUNCES CREAM CHEESE, AT ROOM TEMPERATURE

3 LARGE EGGS, AT ROOM TEMPERATURE

1 TEASPOON PURE VANILLA EXTRACT

FOR THE CHOCOLATE HONEY GLAZE

½ CUP HEAVY CREAM

2 TABLESPOONS HONEY

2 OUNCES SEMISWEET CHOCOLATE, FINELY CHOPPED, OR ⅓ CUP SEMISWEET CHOCOLATE CHIPS

2 OUNCES BITTERSWEET CHOCOLATE, FINELY CHOPPED, OR ⅓ CUP BITTERSWEET CHOCOLATE CHIPS

1 TEASPOON PURE VANILLA EXTRACT

continued

Position a rack in the middle of the oven and preheat the oven to 350°F. Spray a 9-by-5-inch loaf pan with nonstick spray and line with parchment, leaving an overhang on the two long sides of the pan. (This will make it easy to remove the cake from the pan.)

Sift together the flour, baking powder, baking soda, and salt. Set aside.

In a small bowl, combine the sugar and clementine zest. Set aside. (Mixing the zest with the sugar will help distribute the zest more evenly in the batter.)

In the bowl of a stand mixer fitted with the paddle attachment (or in a large mixing bowl, using a handheld mixer), cream the butter and cream cheese together on medium speed for 2 to 3 minutes, until smooth. Gradually add the sugar mixture and then beat on medium-high speed until very light and fluffy, 4 to 5 minutes. Add the eggs one at a time, mixing well after each addition and scraping down the sides of

the bowl with a rubber spatula as necessary. Add the vanilla and mix until combined.

With the mixer on low speed, add the flour mixture in thirds, mixing just until incorporated. Remove the bowl from the mixer and, using the rubber spatula, incorporate any ingredients hiding at the bottom of the bowl, making sure the batter is completely mixed.

Scrape the batter into the prepared pan and gently smooth the top with a spatula. Tap the pan firmly on the counter to remove any air bubbles from the batter.

Bake for 50 to 60 minutes, until a cake tester inserted in the center of the cake comes out clean. Let the cake cool in the pan on a wire rack for about 20 minutes, then remove it from the pan using the parchment, peel off the parchment, and cool completely on the rack.

To make the chocolate honey glaze: In a small saucepan, heat the cream to a gentle boil.

continued

Put the honey in a small mixing bowl and pour the hot cream over the honey. Add both chocolates and stir until completely melted and smooth; the glaze will be shiny and glossy. Stir in the vanilla. Let cool until slightly thickened.

Put the cake on a serving platter and pour the glaze over it, allowing it to drip down on the sides. Let stand until the glaze has set.

The cake can be stored in an airtight container at room temperature for up to 3 days.

LEMON POPPY SEED CAKE WITH LEMON GLAZE

If you love lemons as much as I do, then pucker up, because this cake has more than a twist. The lemon syrup and glaze keep it supermoist, and the flavors get better every day. If you keep it on the kitchen counter, you will be tempted to cut a slice every time you pass it.

1¾ CUPS UNBLEACHED ALL-PURPOSE FLOUR

1 TEASPOON BAKING POWDER, PREFERABLY ALUMINUM-FREE

1 TEASPOON BAKING SODA

¼ TEASPOON FINE SEA SALT

½ POUND (2 STICKS) UNSALTED BUTTER, AT ROOM TEMPERATURE

1 CUP GRANULATED SUGAR

1 TEASPOON PURE VANILLA EXTRACT

3 LARGE EGGS, AT ROOM TEMPERATURE

1 CUP SOUR CREAM, AT ROOM TEMPERATURE

½ CUP POPPY SEEDS

FOR THE SOAKING SYRUP

¾ CUP FRESH LEMON JUICE (FROM 4 TO 5 LEMONS)

¾ CUP GRANULATED SUGAR

FOR THE LEMON GLAZE

1½ CUPS CONFECTIONERS' SUGAR

1 TABLESPOON GRATED LEMON ZEST

3 TABLESPOONS WHOLE MILK

Position a rack in the middle of the oven and preheat the oven to 350°F. Butter a 9-inch springform pan. Line the bottom with parchment and butter it as well. Lightly dust the pan with flour, tapping the pan on the counter to shake out the excess.

Sift together the flour, baking powder, baking soda, and salt. Set aside.

In the bowl of a stand mixer fitted with the paddle attachment (or in a large mixing bowl, using a handheld mixer), cream the butter, sugar, and vanilla together on medium-high speed for 4 to 5 minutes, until light and fluffy. Add the eggs one at a time, mixing well after each addition and scraping down the sides of the bowl with a rubber spatula as necessary.

With the mixer on low speed, gradually add about half of the flour mixture, followed by the sour cream. Add the remaining flour and mix just until incorporated.

Remove the bowl from the mixer and fold in the poppy seeds. Scrape the batter into the prepared pan and spread it evenly with a spatula.

Bake for 50 to 60 minutes, until a cake tester inserted in the center of the cake comes out clean. Let the cake cool in the pan on a wire rack for 15 minutes.

Meanwhile, make the soaking syrup: Combine the lemon juice and sugar in a small nonreactive saucepan and cook over low heat, stirring often, until the sugar

dissolves. Then continue cooking until the syrup turns a deep golden yellow, 3 to 4 minutes. Remove from the heat.

Poke holes all over the cake with a skewer. Pour the soaking syrup over the cake until it is completely moistened. Let the cake stand for at least 10 minutes so the syrup is absorbed. Release the springform ring and remove it, then use a metal spatula to release the cake from the parchment and the bottom of the springform pan and transfer it to a serving platter.

To make the lemon glaze:
In a small bowl, combine the confectioners' sugar, half of the lemon zest, and the milk and whisk until smooth.

Use a spoon to drizzle the glaze over the top of the cake. Sprinkle the remaining lemon zest over the cake. Let stand until the glaze is set.

The cake can be stored in an airtight container at room temperature for up to 5 days.

PINEAPPLE UPSIDE-DOWN CAKE

SERVES 8 TO 12

You can make upside-down cakes with all kinds of fruit, but you just can't beat our take on the classic. We make it in a cast-iron skillet and add bourbon to the salted-caramel pineapple topping. Sprinkle with almonds for added flavor and texture.

FOR THE CARAMEL PINEAPPLE TOPPING

1 PINEAPPLE

6 TABLESPOONS UNSALTED BUTTER

1 CUP PACKED LIGHT BROWN SUGAR

1 TABLESPOON BOURBON (RUM OR VANILLA WORKS TOO)

½ TEASPOON FINE SEA SALT

¾ CUP SLICED ALMONDS, TOASTED

FOR THE CAKE

1⅓ CUPS CAKE FLOUR (NOT SELF-RISING)

2 TEASPOONS BAKING POWDER, PREFERABLY ALUMINUM-FREE

¾ TEASPOON GROUND CINNAMON

1 TEASPOON GROUND GINGER

1 TEASPOON FINE SEA SALT

2 LARGE EGGS, AT ROOM TEMPERATURE

2 TEASPOONS PURE VANILLA EXTRACT

1 CUP GRANULATED SUGAR

8 TABLESPOONS (1 STICK) UNSALTED BUTTER, AT ROOM TEMPERATURE

1 CUP SOUR CREAM

SPECIAL EQUIPMENT

1-INCH ROUND COOKIE CUTTER

Preheat the oven to 350°F.

To prepare the pineapple for the topping: Slice off the top and bottom of the pineapple to create

easy-to-manage flat surfaces. Stand the pineapple up and slice the skin away in long strips following the contours of the fruit, making sure to remove all of the brown eyes. Put the peeled pineapple on its side and cut into ½-inch-thick rounds. Using a 1-inch round cookie cutter, remove the core from each slice. Set the pineapple aside on paper towels.

To make the caramel topping:
Melt the butter in a 10-inch cast-iron skillet over medium heat, or melt it in a 10-inch round cake pan over low heat. Sprinkle the brown sugar, bourbon, and salt over it and cook, stirring occasionally, until the sugar dissolves and the caramel is golden, about 3 minutes. Remove from the heat.

Arrange the sliced pineapple in a circle on top of the caramel mixture, without overlapping the rings, then fill in the center; you can cut the remaining pieces to fill in the gaps if you like. Sprinkle with the toasted almonds.

To make the cake: In a medium bowl, whisk the flour, baking

powder, cinnamon, ginger, and salt together. Set aside.

In a small bowl, whisk the eggs and vanilla together. Set aside.

In the bowl of a stand mixer fitted with the paddle attachment (or in a large mixing bowl, using a handheld mixer), cream the sugar and butter together on medium-high speed for 3 to 5 minutes, until light and fluffy. Gradually add the eggs and vanilla, beating well and scraping down the sides of the bowl with a rubber spatula as necessary, then beat until doubled in volume, about 2 minutes.

Turn the mixer speed down to low and add the flour mixture in thirds, alternating with the sour cream and beginning and ending with the flour.

Remove the bowl from the mixer and use the rubber spatula to incorporate any ingredients hiding at the bottom of the bowl, making sure the batter is completely mixed. Pour the batter over the pineapple and smooth it with a spatula.

Bake for 50 to 60 minutes, until a cake tester inserted in the center of the cake comes out clean. Let the cake cool in the skillet or cake pan for about 30 minutes.

Run a small knife around the edges of the skillet or pan, then place a large serving plate upside down on top and invert the skillet or pan to release the cake onto the plate. Serve warm or at room temperature.

The cake can be stored in an airtight container at room temperature for up to 3 days.

BABY CAKES WITH VANILLA MERINGUE BUTTERCREAM

MAKES 6 SMALL CAKES

A baby cake is a sweet little party cake meant to be enjoyed by one special person for dessert (and perhaps a snack the next day). We inherited our baby cake pans from our mentor, Jane Thompson, but we put our own spin on her idea. We make baby cakes in all flavors based on the season and the occasion and decorate them with roses, paper flags, and vintage toppers. We tinted the cakes shown on the following page in pastel colors. Imagine serving them at your party in your own favorite colors. Decorate the tops of the cakes with edible fresh flowers, buttercream flowers, candy necklaces, or paper flags: you can be as creative and fancy as you like.

3 CUPS CAKE FLOUR
(NOT SELF-RISING)

4 TEASPOONS BAKING POWDER,
PREFERABLY ALUMINUM-FREE

½ TEASPOON FINE SEA SALT

1 CUP WHOLE MILK

1 TEASPOON PURE VANILLA EXTRACT

½ POUND (2 STICKS) UNSALTED
BUTTER, AT ROOM TEMPERATURE

2 CUPS GRANULATED SUGAR

4 LARGE EGGS, SEPARATED,
AT ROOM TEMPERATURE

A FEW DROPS LIQUID GEL FOOD
COLORING (THE COLOR IS YOUR CHOICE;
USE SEVERAL COLORS IF YOU LIKE)

1 RECIPE VANILLA MERINGUE
BUTTERCREAM (RECIPE FOLLOWS)

CONFECTIONERS' SUGAR FOR DUSTING
(OPTIONAL)

SPECIAL EQUIPMENT

SIX 4-INCH ROUND CAKE PANS

continued

Position a rack in the middle of the oven and preheat the oven to 350°F. Butter six 4-inch round cake pans, line the bottoms with parchment, and butter it as well. Lightly dust the pans with flour, tapping the pans on the counter to shake out the excess.

Sift together the flour, baking powder, and salt. Set aside.

In a large measuring cup or a small bowl, whisk the milk and vanilla together. Set aside.

In the bowl of a stand mixer fitted with the paddle attachment (or in a large mixing bowl, using a handheld mixer), cream the butter and sugar on medium-high speed for 3 to 5 minutes, until light and fluffy. Turn the mixer speed down to low and add the egg yolks, beating until thoroughly combined and scraping down the sides of the bowl with a rubber spatula as necessary.

On low speed, add the flour mixture in thirds, alternating with the milk and vanilla and beginning and ending with the flour, mixing until just combined. If using a stand mixer, transfer the batter to another large bowl. Wash and dry the mixer bowl and fit the mixer with the whisk attachment.

Put the egg whites in the clean mixer bowl (or in a clean large mixing bowl) and beat on medium speed with the whisk attachment (or with a handheld mixer with clean beaters) until soft peaks form. Scoop up a little of the egg whites with a rubber spatula and gently stir them into the batter to lighten it and make it easier to fold in the rest of the egg whites. Gently fold in the remaining egg whites until thoroughly incorporated.

Tint the batter to the desired shade with a few drops of food coloring. You can make the batter all one color or use different colors for each cake. It's also fun to make an ombré effect, tinting the batter in one color in a range from light to dark.

Divide the batter among the prepared pans, using about 1 cup for each pan. Gently smooth the tops with a spatula. Tap the pans firmly on the counter to release any air bubbles.

continued

Bake for 20 to 25 minutes, until a cake tester inserted in the center of a cake comes out clean. Let the cakes cool for 15 minutes, then remove from the pans, peel off the parchment, and cool completely on a wire rack.

To assemble the baby cakes: Level the top of each cake with a serrated knife so it is flat. (Eat up—baker's treat!) Carefully slice each cake in half horizontally to make two layers, then flip the cakes over.

Set aside the top half of each cake. Put a small ice cream scoop or a tablespoon of frosting in the middle of each bottom layer and spread it evenly with an offset spatula or a butter knife. Place the top layers back on top. Frost the tops and sides of the cakes (or leave the sides unfrosted and dust with confectioners' sugar).

The cakes are best served at room temperature, but they can be stored wrapped in plastic wrap in the refrigerator for up to 3 days.

Vanilla Meringue Buttercream

MAKES ABOUT 8 CUPS

12 LARGE EGG WHITES

3 CUPS GRANULATED SUGAR

½ TEASPOON FINE SEA SALT

2½ POUNDS UNSALTED BUTTER,
CUT INTO ½-INCH CHUNKS,
AT ROOM TEMPERATURE

1 TABLESPOON PURE VANILLA EXTRACT

SPECIAL EQUIPMENT

CANDY OR INSTANT-READ
THERMOMETER

In the bowl of a stand mixer fitted with the whisk attachment (or in a heatproof metal bowl), whisk the egg whites, sugar, and salt together. Set the bowl over a saucepan of simmering water (do not let the bottom of the bowl touch the water) and cook, whisking constantly, until the sugar is dissolved. The mixture will be warm to the touch and register 140°F on a candy or instant-read thermometer.

Remove the bowl from the heat and attach it to the mixer stand (or use a handheld mixer). Beat on high speed until stiff peaks form and the meringue cools to room temperature, 3 to 5 minutes.

Once the mixture has cooled to room temperature, replace the whisk with the paddle attachment and begin adding the butter. Add the butter chunks a few at a time, waiting for them to be incorporated before adding more and scraping down the sides of the bowl as needed. Don't worry if the mixture begins to look curdled; if that happens, slow down and make sure you are completely incorporating the butter before adding more. When all of the butter has been added, add the vanilla and beat for another 1 to 2 minutes. The frosting should be smooth, thick, and glossy.

Use immediately. Or store it in an airtight container in the refrigerator for up to 1 week. To use buttercream that has been chilled, see the Tip on page 38.

FESTIVE YULE LOG

SERVES 12 TO 16

Our Southern spin on the traditional French bûche de Noël is made with chiffon cake, espresso buttercream, and a rich chocolate buttercream, and it's decorated with sugared rosemary sprigs and cranberries, and pistachio "moss"; you can use some or all of these and any other festive additions you like. This recipe is a showstopping centerpiece for your Christmas table.

¼ CUP VEGETABLE OIL

4 LARGE EGGS, SEPARATED, AT ROOM TEMPERATURE

1½ TEASPOONS PURE VANILLA EXTRACT

1 CUP PLUS 2 TABLESPOONS UNBLEACHED ALL-PURPOSE FLOUR

1 TEASPOON BAKING POWDER, PREFERABLY ALUMINUM-FREE

¾ CUP GRANULATED SUGAR

½ TEASPOON FINE SEA SALT

2 LARGE EGG WHITES

¼ TEASPOON CREAM OF TARTAR OR FRESH LEMON JUICE

FOR THE COFFEE SYRUP

¼ CUP HOT FRESHLY BREWED COFFEE

¼ CUP GRANULATED SUGAR

1 RECIPE WHIPPED ESPRESSO BUTTERCREAM (RECIPE FOLLOWS)

1 RECIPE CLASSIC CHOCOLATE BUTTERCREAM (RECIPE FOLLOWS)

SUGARED ROSEMARY AND CRANBERRIES AND PISTACHIO MOSS (SEE PAGE 101) AND/OR OTHER DECORATIONS OF YOUR CHOICE

SPECIAL EQUIPMENT

PLASTIC DRINKING STRAW

Position a rack in the lower third of the oven and preheat the oven to 325°F. Line a baking sheet with parchment.

In a small bowl, whisk the oil, egg yolks, ⅓ cup plus 1 tablespoon water, and vanilla together. Set aside.

Sift together the flour and baking powder into a large bowl. Add ½ cup plus 1 tablespoon of the sugar and the salt and whisk to combine. Make a well in the center of the flour mixture, add the egg yolk mixture, and whisk briskly until very smooth.

In the clean bowl of a stand mixer fitted with the whisk attachment (or in a clean large bowl, using a handheld mixer), beat all the egg whites on medium speed until frothy. Add the cream of tartar and beat on medium-high speed until the whites hold soft peaks. Slowly add the remaining 3 tablespoons sugar and beat until the whites hold firm, shiny peaks.

Using a rubber spatula, scoop about one-third of the whites into the yolk mixture and fold in gently. Gently but thoroughly fold in the remaining whites just until combined.

Pour the batter into the prepared pan, smoothing the top with an offset spatula. Bake for 20 to 25 minutes, until the cake is just set to the touch. Let cool completely on a rack. The cake can be stored wrapped in plastic wrap in the refrigerator for up to 3 days.

To make the coffee syrup: In a small bowl, mix together the coffee and sugar, stirring until the sugar dissolves. Set aside.

To assemble the log: Invert the cake onto a piece of parchment and peel off the top sheet of parchment. Using a pastry brush, moisten the cake with the coffee syrup. With an offset spatula, spread the espresso buttercream evenly over the cake, leaving a 1-inch border on the long sides. Starting from a long side, roll up the cake, using the parchment to help you lift and roll it evenly and tightly. The cake may crack as you roll, but just continue to roll. Refrigerate the rolled cake until the buttercream is firm, about 2 hours.

To frost and decorate the log: Using a sharp knife, trim off the ends of the log, about ½ inch on each end. Cut a 6-inch piece from one end of the log and cut it diagonally in half.

Place the log seam side down on a serving platter (you can keep the edges of the platter clean by sliding strips of parchment under the cake while you frost it). Use a small offset spatula to place 2 dollops of the chocolate buttercream on the top

to anchor the "branches." Place one branch slanted side up on top of the log. Cut a plastic straw in half and insert one piece into the bough to secure it, then cut off the end of the straw so it doesn't show. Place the other branch on the side of the log, next to the top "bough," attach with the other piece of straw, and trim the straw. Frost the log and branches with the remaining frosting.

Use the recipes below or pull out the sparkly dragées and edible flowers and decorate your yule log as you please.

The log can be stored in an airtight container in the refrigerator for up to 5 days.

YULE LOG DECORATIONS

Sugared Rosemary and Cranberries: Combine ¾ cup granulated sugar and ½ cup water in a small saucepan and bring to a boil over medium heat.

Stir to dissolve the sugar. Set aside to cool.

Once the syrup is cool, drop in about 4 fresh rosemary sprigs and 1 cup cranberries, then remove with a slotted spoon, draining them well. Roll in extra-fine sugar. Spread out on a baking sheet lined with parchment and set aside to dry for at least 2 hours. Store, uncovered, at room temperature for up to 4 days.

Pistachio Moss: Put ¼ cup shelled pistachios in a small blender or coffee grinder and pulse until they look like powdery "moss." Store in an airtight container in the refrigerator for up to 2 weeks or freeze for up to 1 month.

Whipped Espresso Buttercream

MAKES ABOUT 3½ CUPS

¼ CUP SIFTED ALL-PURPOSE FLOUR

1 CUP WHOLE MILK

1½ TEASPOONS STRONG ESPRESSO
(FROM A SHOT, OR MADE FROM
POWDERED ESPRESSO)

1 TEASPOON PURE VANILLA EXTRACT

½ POUND (2 STICKS) UNSALTED
BUTTER, AT ROOM TEMPERATURE

1 CUP GRANULATED SUGAR

Combine the flour, ¼ cup of the milk, the espresso, and vanilla in a small heavy saucepan and whisk until blended. Set the pan over medium heat and gradually add the remaining ¾ cup milk, whisking constantly, then cook, whisking, until the mixture comes to a low boil. Reduce the heat to low and whisk until the mixture begins to thicken and starts to "burp," 2 to 3 minutes.

Transfer the mixture to a small heatproof bowl and stir occasionally as it cools to keep it lump-free. If you do get a few lumps, don't worry—you can whisk the mixture to dissolve the lumps, or pass it through a fine-mesh sieve. (You can put the mixture in the refrigerator for 10 minutes to speed up the process.)

In the bowl of a stand mixer fitted with the whisk attachment (or in a large mixing bowl, using a handheld mixer), beat the butter on medium speed for 3 minutes, until smooth and creamy. Gradually add the sugar and then beat on high speed for 5 to 7 minutes until the mixture is light and fluffy.

Reduce the speed and gradually add the milk mixture, then beat on medium-high speed for 4 to 5 minutes until thick and creamy.

Use immediately. Or store in an airtight container in the refrigerator for up to 3 days. To use buttercream that has been chilled, see the Tip on page 38.

Classic Chocolate Buttercream

MAKES ABOUT 3 CUPS

4 OUNCES SEMISWEET CHOCOLATE, FINELY CHOPPED, OR ⅔ CUP SEMISWEET CHOCOLATE CHIPS

12 TABLESPOONS (1½ STICKS) UNSALTED BUTTER, AT ROOM TEMPERATURE

1 TABLESPOON WHOLE MILK

½ TEASPOON PURE VANILLA EXTRACT

1½ CUPS CONFECTIONERS' SUGAR, SIFTED

Put the chocolate in a heatproof bowl, set it over a saucepan of simmering water (do not let the bottom of the bowl touch the water), and stir occasionally until the chocolate is completely melted. Set the chocolate aside to cool until tepid.

In the bowl of a stand mixer fitted with the paddle attachment (or in a medium mixing bowl, using a handheld mixer), beat the butter on medium speed for 2 to 3 minutes, until smooth and creamy. Add the milk, mixing until completely blended. Add the cooled chocolate and mix until completely incorporated, scraping down the sides of the bowl with a rubber spatula as necessary. Beat in the vanilla. With the mixer on low speed, gradually add the confectioners' sugar and then continue beating until the buttercream is smooth, thick, and glossy.

The frosting can be stored in an airtight container at room temperature for up to 2 days.

RESOURCES

The following companies and vendors supply Back in the Day Bakery with high-quality ingredients and baking supplies. Griff and I encourage you to check them out for your own baking needs.

Anson Mills
(803) 467-4122
ansonmills.com

An artisanal mill in South Carolina that hand-mills grits, rice, cornmeal, and specialty flours from organic heirloom grains.

Batdorf & Bronson
Coffee Roasters
(800) 955-5282
batdorfcoffee.com

Sustainable and fair-trade single-origin and blend roasters.

Chocosphere
(503) 692-3323
chocosphere.com

A supplier of fine chocolate from around the world.

Etsy
etsy.com

An online community of artisans buying and selling handcrafted and vintage items.

Everyday Is a Holiday
everyday-is-a-holiday
.blogspot.com

Art inspired by baked goods and vintage treasures. We have quite a collection, including the "Keep Calm and Have a Cupcake" sign that proudly hangs in our bakery.

Fabrika
2 East Liberty Street
Savannah, GA 31401
(912) 236-1122
fabrikafinefabrics.com

Fabrics, notions, and gifts.

Habersham Antique Market & Collectibles
**2502 Habersham Street
Savannah, GA 31401
(912) 238-5908**

An antiques mall in midtown Savannah that features a wide array of vintage treasures.

Herriott Grace
herriottgrace.com

A supplier of handcrafted cake plates and wooden things.

Jacobsen Salt Co.
**(503) 719-4973
jacobsensalt.com**

Beyond their flake and kosher sea salts, this nationally recognized brand also offers a wide variety of seasonings, spice blends, and other pantry staples.

Katie Runnels
**(479) 684-6885
theconstantgatherer.com**

A supplier of vintage treasures, Katie, a mixed-media artist, is inspired by her love of family and traditions, vintage wares, and Cheryl's buttercream frosting.

King Arthur Flour
**(800) 827-6836
kingarthurflour.com**

An employee-owned company that has been making pure flours (including almond) for more than two hundred years and an essential source for baking supplies.

Layer Cake Shop
layercakeshop.com

A one-stop shop for adding vintage charm to homemade cakes.

Nordic Ware
**(877) 466-7342
nordicware.com**

Known for creating the Bundt pan, this family-owned business produces quality bakeware and kitchen tools that will become family heirlooms.

Oh Happy Day
shop.ohhappyday.com

Oh, let the party begin. This is my favorite one-stop shop for all things festive and fun. Looking for cake toppers, favors and gifts, tabletop accessories, or confetti balloons? You will find it all right here.

Savannah's Clay Spot
**1305 Barnard Street
Savannah, GA 31401
(912) 509-4647
savannahsclayspot.com**

A great source for cake plates and other wares by local Savannah potter Lisa Alvarez Bradley.

Scharffen Berger
**(855) 972-0511
shop.scharffenberger.com**

This artisan manufacturer offers a large selection of balanced and complex chocolates made from the finest cacao.

Shop Sweet Lulu
**702 Center Road
Frankfort, IL 60423
(815) 464-6264
shopsweetlulu.com**

Lovely food packaging and party-styling essentials from all over the world.

The Spice House
**(312) 676-2414
thespicehouse.com**

Merchants of the highest quality hand-selected and hand-prepared spices and herbs, including cardamom.

Terra Cotta
**34 Barnard Street
Savannah, GA 31401
(912) 236-6150
terracottasavannah.com**

Great gifts and home accessories.

Terrain
**(877) 583-7724
shopterrain.com**

This Philadelphia-area store and online boutique sells salts, heirloom seeds, canning jars, and treasures for the home.

Williams-Sonoma
**(877) 812-6235
williams-sonoma.com**

A specialty retailer of gourmet cookware and kitchen tools.

INDEX

Note: Page numbers in *italics* refer to illustrations.

Alabama Lane Cake, 61–64, *62*
Angel Food Cake with Whipped Cream and
  Berries, 76–79, *77*
applesauce: Spice Cake with Butterscotch
  Icing, 71–73
apricots: Spice Cake with Butterscotch Icing,
  71–73

Baby Cakes with Vanilla Meringue
  Buttercream, 93–97, *94*
bananas: Hummingbird Cake with Cream
  Cheese Frosting, 29–31, *30*
bourbon:
  Alabama Lane Cake, 61–64, *62*
  Caramel Pineapple Topping, 89–92, *90*
Brown Sugar Bundt Cake with Butterscotch
  Glaze, 65–66, *67*
butter:
  creaming, 13
  room temperature, 10
buttercreams:
  chilled (tip), 38
  Chocolate Buttercream, 19
  Classic Chocolate Buttercream, *100*, 103
  Coconut Buttercream, 23
  Italian Meringue Buttercream, 37–38
  Lemon Meringue Buttercream, *58*, 60
  Vanilla Meringue Buttercream, *94*, 97
  variations, 38
  Whipped Buttercream Frosting, 53
  Whipped Espresso Buttercream, *100*, 102
buttermilk:
  Cakette Party Cake with Italian Meringue
    Buttercream, 34–38, *35*
  Chocolate Cream Cake with Dark Chocolate
    Ganache, *50*, 51–55
  Cocoa-Cola Cake with Chocolate Icing, *80*,
    81–82

Butterscotch Glaze, 65, 66, *67*
Butterscotch Icing, 73

Cakette Party Cake with Italian Meringue
  Buttercream, 34–38, *35*
Caramel Cake with Salted Caramel Frosting,
  43–49, *44*
Caramel Pineapple Topping, 89–92, *90*
Carrot Cake with Spiced Cream Cheese
  Frosting, 32–33
chocolate:
  Chocolate Buttercream, 19
  Chocolate Cream Cake with Dark Chocolate
    Ganache, *50*, 51–55
  Chocolate Glaze, 74, 75
  Chocolate Heaven with Chocolate
    Buttercream, *16*, 17–19
  Chocolate Honey Glaze, 83–86, *84*
  Chocolate Icing, *80*, 81, 82
  Classic Chocolate Buttercream, *100*, 103
  Dark Chocolate Ganache, *54*, 55
  Deep, Dark Flourless Chocolate Cake, *68*,
    69–70
  Mexican Spice Cake with Chocolate Glaze,
    74–75
Clementine Pound Cake with Chocolate Honey
  Glaze, 83–86, *84*
Coca-Cola: Cocoa-Cola Cake with Chocolate
  Icing, *80*, 81–82
cocoa:
  Chocolate Cream Cake with Dark Chocolate
    Ganache, *50*, 51–55
  Chocolate Icing, *80*, 81, 82
  Cocoa-Cola Cake with Chocolate Icing, *80*,
    81–82
  Mexican Spice Cake with Chocolate Glaze,
    74–75
  Red Velvet Cake with Cream Cheese
    Frosting, 25–28, *27*
coconut:
  Alabama Lane Cake, 61–64, *62*

Coconut Cake with Coconut Buttercream, *20*, 21–23
coffee:
  Chocolate Cream Cake with Dark Chocolate Ganache, *50*, 51–55
  Chocolate Heaven with Chocolate Buttercream, *16*, 17–19
  Coffee Syrup, 98, 99
  Dark Chocolate Ganache, *54*, 55
  Deep, Dark Flourless Chocolate Cake, *68*, 69–70
  Whipped Espresso Buttercream, *100*, 102
cranberries: Sugared Rosemary and Cranberries, *100*, 101
Cream, Whipped, *77*, 79
Cream Cheese Frosting, *27*, 28, *30*
currants: Carrot Cake with Spiced Cream Cheese Frosting, 32–33

eggs:
  Alabama Lane Cake, 61–64, *62*
  functions of, 11
  Italian Meringue Buttercream, 37–38
  Lemon Meringue Buttercream, *58*, 60
  room temperature, 10
  Vanilla Meringue Buttercream, *94*, 97
equipment, 14–15
espresso: Whipped Espresso Buttercream, *100*, 102

Festive Yule Log, 98–103, *100*
flour, measuring, 13
flourless cake: Deep, Dark Flourless Chocolate Cake, *68*, 69–70
frostings:
  Alabama Lane Cake, 61–64, *62*
  Cream Cheese Frosting, *27*, 28, *30*
  "crumb coat," 49
  Salted Caramel Frosting, *44*, 49
  Spiced Cream Cheese Frosting, 28
  Whipped Buttercream Frosting, 53
ganache:
Dark Chocolate Ganache, *54*, 55
glazes:
  Butterscotch Glaze, 65, 66, *67*

Chocolate Glaze, 74, 75
  Chocolate Honey Glaze, 83–86, *84*
  Lemon Glaze, 87–88
  Simple Syrup, 24
Grand Marnier: Deep, Dark Flourless Chocolate Cake, *68*, 69–70

Hummingbird Cake with Cream Cheese Frosting, 29–31, *30*

icings:
  Butterscotch Icing, 73
  Chocolate Icing, *80*, 81, 82
ingredients, 11
Italian Meringue Buttercream, 37–38

Janie Q's Lemon Cake with Lemon Meringue Buttercream, 56–60, *58*

leavening agents, 11
lemon:
  Janie Q's Lemon Cake with Lemon Meringue Buttercream, 56–60, *58*
  Lemon Curd, 56, 57, 59
  Lemon Glaze, 87–88
  Lemon Meringue Buttercream, *58*, 60
  Lemon Poppy Seed Cake with Lemon Glaze, 87–88

marshmallows: Cocoa-Cola Cake with Chocolate Icing, *80*, 81–82
Mexican Spice Cake with Chocolate Glaze, 74–75
mise en place, 8

nuts:
  Alabama Lane Cake, 61–64, *62*
  Caramel Pineapple Topping, 89–92, *90*
  Carrot Cake with Spiced Cream Cheese Frosting, 32–33
  Chocolate Icing, *80*, 81, 82
  Hummingbird Cake with Cream Cheese Frosting, 29–31, *30*
  Spice Cake with Butterscotch Icing, 71–73

pineapple:
  Hummingbird Cake with Cream Cheese
    Frosting, 29–31, *30*
  Pineapple Upside-Down Cake, 89–92, *90*
Pistachio Moss, 101
poppy seeds: Lemon Poppy Seed Cake with
    Lemon Glaze, 87–88
pound cake: Clementine Pound Cake with
    Chocolate Honey Glaze, 83–86, *84*

raisins: Alabama Lane Cake, 61–64, *62*
Red Velvet Cake with Cream Cheese Frosting,
    25–28, *27*
resources, 105–7

Salted Caramel Frosting, *44*, 49
Salted Caramel Sauce, 46–48, *47*
Simple Syrup, 24
sour cream:
  Chocolate Heaven with Chocolate
    Buttercream, *16*, 17–19

Lemon Poppy Seed Cake with Lemon Glaze,
    87–88
  Pineapple Upside-Down Cake, 89–92, *90*
Spice Cake with Butterscotch Icing, 71–73
Spiced Cream Cheese Frosting, 28
spices, 15
Sugared Rosemary and Cranberries, *100*, 101

temperature, 8, 10
Tiered Celebration Cake, 39–42, *40*
tool kit, 14–15

Upside-Down Cake, Pineapple, 89–92, *90*

Vanilla Meringue Buttercream, *94*, 97

Whipped Cream, *77*, 79

Yule Log, Festive, 98–103, *100*

CONVERSION CHARTS

Here are rounded-off equivalents between the metric system and the traditional systems that are used in the United States to measure weight and volume.

FRACTIONS	DECIMALS
⅛	.125
¼	.25
⅓	.33
⅜	.375
½	.5
⅝	.625
⅔	.67
¾	.75
⅞	.875

WEIGHTS

US/UK	METRIC
¼ oz	7 g
½ oz	15 g
1 oz	30 g
2 oz	55 g
3 oz	85 g
4 oz	110 g
5 oz	140 g
6 oz	170 g
7 oz	200 g
8 oz (½ lb)	225 g
9 oz	250 g
10 oz	280 g
11 oz	310 g
12 oz	340 g
13 oz	370 g
14 oz	400 g
15 oz	425 g
16 oz (1 lb)	455 g

VOLUME

AMERICAN	IMPERIAL	METRIC
¼ tsp		1.25 ml
½ tsp		2.5 ml
1 tsp		5 ml
½ Tbsp (1½ tsp)		7.5 ml
1 Tbsp (3 tsp)		15 ml
¼ cup (4 Tbsp)	2 fl oz	60 ml
⅓ cup (5 Tbsp)	2½ fl oz	75 ml
½ cup (8 Tbsp)	4 fl oz	125 ml
⅔ cup (10 Tbsp)	5 fl oz	150 ml
¾ cup (12 Tbsp)	6 fl oz	175 ml
1 cup (16 Tbsp)	8 fl oz	250 ml
1¼ cups	10 fl oz	300 ml
1½ cups	12 fl oz	350 ml
2 cups (1 pint)	16 fl oz	500 ml
2½ cups	20 fl oz (1 pint)	625 ml
5 cups	40 fl oz (1 qt)	1.25 l

OVEN TEMPERATURES

	°F	°C	GAS MARK
very cool	250–275	130–140	½–1
cool	300	148	2
warm	325	163	3
moderate	350	177	4
moderately hot	375–400	190–204	5–6
hot	425	218	7
very hot	450–475	232–245	8–9

°C/F TO °F/C CONVERSION CHART

°C/F	°C	°F	°C/F	°C	°F	°C/F	°C	°F	°C/F	°C	°F
90	32	194	220	104	428	350	177	662	480	249	896
100	38	212	230	110	446	360	182	680	490	254	914
110	43	230	240	116	464	370	188	698	500	260	932
120	49	248	250	121	482	380	193	716	510	266	950
130	54	266	260	127	500	390	199	734	520	271	968
140	60	284	270	132	518	400	204	752	530	277	986
150	66	302	280	138	536	410	210	770	540	282	1,004
160	71	320	290	143	554	420	216	788	550	288	1,022
170	77	338	300	149	572	430	221	806			
180	82	356	310	154	590	440	227	824			
190	88	374	320	160	608	450	232	842			
200	93	392	330	166	626	460	238	860			
210	99	410	340	171	644	470	243	878			

Example: If your temperature is 90°F, your conversion is 32°C; if your temperature is 90°C, your conversion is 194°F.

Library of Congress Cataloging-in-Publication Data.

Names: Day, Cheryl, author. | Day, Griffith, author.
Title: The Artisanal kitchen. Party cakes / Cheryl Day and Griffith Day.
Description: New York : Artisan, a division of Workman Publishing Co., Inc. [2018] |
    Includes an index.
Identifiers: LCCN 2018003631 | ISBN 9781579658595 (hardcover : alk. paper)
Subjects: LCSH: Cake. | Parties. | LCGFT: Cookbooks.
Classification: LCC TX771 .D39 2018 | DDC 641.86/53—dc23
LC record available at https://lccn.loc.gov/2018003631

Design by Erica Heitman-Ford

Artisan books are available at special discounts when purchased in bulk for premiums
and sales promotions as well as for fund-raising or educational use. Special editions or
book excerpts also can be created to specification. For details, contact the Special Sales
Director at the address below, or send an e-mail to specialmarkets@workman.com.

For speaking engagements, contact speakersbureau@workman.com

Published by Artisan
A division of Workman Publishing Co., Inc.
225 Varick Street
New York, NY 10014-4381
artisanbooks.com

Artisan is a registered trademark of Workman Publishing Co., Inc.

This book has been adapted from *The Back in the Day Bakery Cookbook* (Artisan, 2012)
and *Back in the Day Bakery Made with Love* (Artisan, 2015).

Published simultaneously in Canada by Thomas Allen & Son, Limited

Printed in China
First printing, July 2018

10 9 8 7 6 5 4 3 2 1